This is a volume in the Arno Press Series

NATIONAL BUREAU
OF
ECONOMIC RESEARCH
PUBLICATIONS
IN REPRINT

See last pages of this volume
for a complete list of titles.

THE GROWTH OF AMERICAN TRADE UNIONS 1880–1923

By

LEO WOLMAN

ARNO PRESS
A New York Times Company
New York – 1975

Editorial Supervision: Eve Nelson
Reprint Edition 1975 by Arno Press Inc.

NATIONAL BUREAU OF ECONOMIC RESEARCH
PUBLICATIONS IN REPRINT
ISBN for complete set: 0-405-07572-3
See last pages of this volume for titles.

Manufactured in the United States of America

Library of Congress Cataloging in Publication Data

Wolman, Leo, 1890-1961.
The growth of American trade unions, 1880-1923.

(National Bureau of Economic Research publications in reprint)
Reprint of the ed. published by National Bureau of Economic Research, New York, which was issued as no. 6 of the Bureau's Publications.
1. Trade-unions--United States--History. I. Title. II. Series. III. Series: National Bureau of Economic Research. General series ; no. 6.
HD6508.W6 1975 331.88'0973 75-19738
ISBN 0-405-07615-0

PUBLICATIONS OF THE NATIONAL BUREAU OF
ECONOMIC RESEARCH, INCORPORATED

No. 6

THE GROWTH OF AMERICAN TRADE UNIONS, 1880-1923

THE GROWTH OF AMERICAN TRADE UNIONS 1880–1923

By

LEO WOLMAN

OF THE STAFF OF THE
NATIONAL BUREAU OF ECONOMIC RESEARCH, INCORPORATED

With a Foreword by

WESLEY C. MITCHELL

NEW YORK
NATIONAL BUREAU OF ECONOMIC
RESEARCH, INC.
1924

PRINTED IN THE U. S. A.

J. J. LITTLE & IVES COMPANY

FOREWORD

The first task essayed by the National Bureau of Economic Research was to determine as accurately as might be the size and distribution of the income produced and consumed by the people of the United States. As our estimates neared completion, we realized that they involved us in a series of new problems. Among these problems one of the most obvious was the considerable fluctuations in the national income from year to year which our figures showed. What produces these fluctuations? How are they shared by the various classes of income receivers—farmers, wage earners, investors, business men? How does a rise or fall of money income one year react upon consumption and production—that is, upon the well-being of the population and the income of future years?

It seemed incumbent upon the National Bureau to answer these questions if it could. They grew out of its own work, they were of grave importance to the country, they could be attacked by quantitative methods—in short, they were questions of precisely the sort which the National Bureau had been organized to treat. Accordingly, after our first two reports had been published, giving estimates of the income of the country in 1909 to 1919, the Executive Committee of the Board of Directors authorized the staff to make a new series of investigations dealing with fluctuations in income. In these studies especial attention was to be given to those alternating expansions and contractions of activity which are known as business cycles.

Soon after this program had been adopted, Secretary Hoover asked the National Bureau to organize an investigation for a committee appointed by the President's Conference on Unemployment. This committee was charged to report upon methods of preventing the recurrence of such periods of widespread unemployment as had led President Harding to call the Conference of 1921. The National Bureau's task was to collect and present materials which might be of use, not only to the committee, but also to all others interested in mitigating crises and depressions. Of course, changes in the number of men at work for wages are the chief immediate cause of fluctuations in the size and in the distribution of the national income. In responding to Secretary Hoover's call, the National Bureau was beginning to carry out the plans it had already laid.

The two reports which grew out of this connection—*Business Cycles and Unemployment* and *Employment, Hours, and Earnings in Prosperity and Depression*, published in 1923—presented our first results in this field of research.

A second venture in this field was undertaken in 1923 at the instance of the National Research Council. The Laura Spelman Rockefeller Memorial had enabled the Council to inaugurate a series of researches in the scientific problems of human migration. We were asked to participate by investigating the bearings of migration upon labor supply in the United States. A report upon this subject, prepared by Dr. Harry Jerome, is nearing completion and will soon be published under the title *Migration and the Business Cycle*.

The present volume on *The Growth of American Trade Unions, 1880–1923*, is another outgrowth of the program framed in 1922. Its relevance is clear. The trade union movement affects productivity and affects wages—that is, it affects both the size and the distribution of the national income. The varying membership of trade unions from year to year, and the proportions of all wage earners who are thus organized—the leading subjects of the following chapters—concern the general public only less than they concern employers and employees. In determining the facts on these heads as accurately as the materials permit, the National Bureau is following its policy of providing men of all shades of opinion with objective knowledge of the conditions which confront them. As in all our work, so here: we confine ourselves to stating the facts as we find them. With opinions about the promise or the danger to American life from the growth of trade unions we have no concern as an organization of investigators.

While it is devoted to "fact finding," the National Bureau has done much of its work on the frontier of statistics. The growth of a science, like the growth of a nation on a new continent, involves repeated rough explorations of territory which cannot be mapped with precision for years to come. We have not hesitated to meet the risks which all explorers take when we have thought the public interest would be served by venturing into territory that is but vaguely known. In the present volume we are making a fresh reconnaissance of ground most of which has already been traversed by others; but even our survey makes no claim to precision. The figures it gives are approximations rather than accurate determinations. That is all that figures can be in this territory now; for the statistics of membership in trade unions and still more the census tables of occupations are defective. The author, Dr. Leo Wolman, shows what the chief defects are, and how they leave a margin of uncertainty around many of his results. We believe, however, that these results are as dependable as can be reached in the present state of the original data. We believe further that knowledge is better served by publishing these carefully made approximations than by doing nothing until the data have become satisfactory. The wait might be a long one.

It should be added that the study of trade union membership is a necessary preliminary to further work which Dr. Wolman is carrying on for the National Bureau. Our volumes on *Income in the United States* show that wage earners are much the most numerous class of income receivers, and that wages is much the largest of the income streams. In treating fluctuations of income, we therefore wish to learn all we can about this crucially important factor. Dr. Wolman, whose experience has given him especial competence in such inquiries, is studying wages at large. One of his themes is the fluctuations of labor costs to employers, a difficult problem which involves joint consideration of wage rates and of efficiency. A second theme is the fluctuations in the retail demand for consumers' goods, also a difficult problem involving joint consideration of wage rates and volume of employment. A third theme is the fluctuations in real wages, which involves joint consideration not merely of money earnings and cost of living, but also of leisure.

What results Dr. Wolman will succeed in getting out of the voluminous yet fragmentary data cannot be foretold. If his efforts prosper as we hope, the present volume will be followed at intervals by two or three others, which will make use of the figures of trade union membership here presented in connection with larger bodies of fresh materials. All these labor studies, together with Dr. Harry Jerome's work on migration, Dr. F. R. Macaulay's investigation of bond yields and discount rates which is nearing completion, and Mr. Willard L. Thorp's collection of business annals and statistics will contribute toward the preparation of the general treatise upon business cycles which the National Bureau has under way.

WESLEY C. MITCHELL.

ACKNOWLEDGMENTS

This study would not have been possible without the coöperation of the many officials of trade unions, who opened their records to the National Bureau of Economic Research and patiently replied to innumerable requests for further information. Miss Florence Thorne, Secretary to Mr. Samuel Gompers, was of great assistance in pointing out defects in the data and in making available unused sources of new data. The burdensome and skilled task of constructing the tables and the charts, checking the statistics, and seeing the book through the press was accomplished by Miss Elizabeth W. Putnam, of the Staff of the National Bureau. Mr. H. K. Herwitz and Mrs. Dorothy J. Orchard, of the Research Department of the Amalgamated Clothing Workers of America, were from the beginning helpful with criticism and suggestion. The author wishes particularly to acknowledge his indebtedness to Professor George E. Barnett, of Johns Hopkins University, under whose direction he completed, in 1915, his first study of the statistics of American trade unions.

LEO WOLMAN.

CONTENTS

LIST OF TABLES IN THE TEXT

LIST OF CHARTS

LIST OF TABLES IN APPENDIX

THE GROWTH OF AMERICAN TRADE UNIONS, 1880–1923

CHAPTER I

INTRODUCTION

This study of the changes in the membership of American trade unions in the past 44 years was undertaken as one of a series of inquiries into the social and economic effects of changing conditions of business. As progress was made in the collection of materials, it became clear that the treatment of these materials should not be limited to a discussion of the influence of the business cycle on the movement of trade union membership. In this range of social phenomena factors other than business prosperity or depression sometimes play a controlling rôle. Public policy, developments in foreign countries, great strikes, all exert a powerful influence on the rise and decline in the membership of trade unions. The detailed facts of the changes in the numbers affiliated with labor organizations and their analysis cannot now be found in any single convenient place. For these reasons a more elaborate collection of statistics was made than would have been required for a simple analysis of the relation between the business cycle and changes in union membership.

Prior to this investigation several comprehensive studies of the same question had already been made. Professor George E. Barnett published in 1916 and in 1922 two articles on the growth of labor organization in the United States from 1897 to 1914 and from 1914 to 1920.[1] In 1916, also, the present author published a paper on the extent of labor organization in the United States in 1910, in which the membership of trade unions in that year

[1] "Growth of Labor Organization in the United States, 1897–1914," *Quarterly Journal of Economics*, Vol. XXX, Aug., 1916; "The Present Position of American Trade Unionism," *American Economic Review*, Supplement, Vol. XII, No. 1, March, 1922.

was compared with the numbers gainfully employed in industry.[1] This study carries the earlier data through the year 1923 and presents an account of the size of the labor movement in the period from 1880 to 1897. The tables from Professor Barnett's two earlier papers are reprinted here. They have, however, been modified in several important respects. Where, in a few instances, trade unions have been able to supply the statistics of membership from their own records, these figures were used in place of the records of the American Federation of Labor. Several unions, whose membership was not available to Professor Barnett, have now submitted their figures and they are included in the revised tables. The new tables indicate also for each union and for each year their state of affiliation with or independence of the American Federation of Labor. In order, furthermore, to indicate the general nature of the growth or decline of the American labor movement before 1897, incomplete series of membership statistics are presented for the period from 1880 to 1897. The analysis, likewise, of the extent of organization among occupied persons was brought up to date by comparing the membership of trade unions in 1920 with the occupation statistics of the decennial census of that year. Here again the necessities of comparability required the reproduction, in revised form, of two tables on the extent of organization in 1910.

In the United States as elsewhere there are a substantial number of organizations, exclusively composed of workmen, which more or less closely resemble the trade union both in structure and function. Decision as to their inclusion in this study must of necessity be in large measure arbitrary. No attempt has been made to draft a refined definition of a bona fide trade union or labor organization. Such associations as company unions and works councils, which are not affiliated with existing labor organizations, are commonly and widely regarded as different from the trade union, for a variety of reasons which need not be the subject of inquiry here. This prevailing view is accepted as the basis of choice and under it all company unions are excluded from the present

[1] "The Extent of Labor Organization in the United States in 1910," *Quarterly Journal of Economics*, Vol. XXX, May, 1916. See also Leo Wolman, "The Extent of Trade Unionism," *Annals of the American Academy of Political and Social Science*, January, 1917.

study. It should be noted, however, that the distinction in any case between trade unions and other workmen's associations is frequentlv a vague and changing one. What is today a company union may tomorrow have all of the characteristics of a trade union. Thus in their early history several of the railroad brotherhoods were forbidden by their own laws the use of the strike. While company unions and like associations, which have in the last decade experienced a rapid growth in this country, are similarly undergoing radical modification in their habits and conduct, it is clear that their course is on the whole still shaped by forces other than those which affect the strength of trade unions. The membership of company unions, then, is properly the subject for separate and independent inquiry.

During, roughly, the last half century the membership of the American trade unions has twice reached striking peaks, from which it has later descended. The first peak was achieved in 1887 when membership rose to about 1,000,000 and the second in 1920 when it exceeded 5,000,000. In each case the labor movement failed to hold its maximum numbers. Following 1887 the losses suffered by labor unions were so great that membership in the early nineties was probably little more than a few hundred thousand; and since 1920 the unions have lost more than one and a quarter millions. The two situations are not, however, analogous. The labor movement of the eighties was a labor movement in the process of discovering itself; it was torn by internal conflict; and it was engaged in finding the form and methods of effective organization. The resolution of these forces of internal dissension and the realization of some concensus of opinion regarding a program of development left the movement in the middle nineties small, but started on a new career. Thereafter the rise in members has been almost continuous and has always been large. The first great break came with the industrial depression of 1921 and has lasted for most unions through 1923. In this last year, however, the labor movement has still a membership of close to 4,000,000, roughly 1,000,000 greater than it was in the years before the World War and more than 3,000,000 above the membership in 1897 when the movement may be said to have entered upon its present phase.

In the years before the war, when membership rose from about 450,000 to 2,750,000, the gains from year to year were made by the craft unions in the building trades, steam railroad and printing industries, and by the coming into power of the United Mine Workers. In fact, during almost the whole of this period, nearly half of the total membership was to be found in the transportation and building groups, while the rest were scattered over the entire range of industries and services. Only in a few places like the coal mines and glass and stone industries was there a like concentration of union membership.

This condition was changed quite radically in the years from 1915 to 1920 by the extensive spread of unionism among the semi-skilled and unskilled and into industries, hitherto almost totally unorganized. Unions in the textile industry and in packing and slaughter houses grew by leaps and bounds. The metal unions increased fourfold by accessions in the metal industries proper and in railroad shops. In steam transportation the striking gains were made by unions, only slightly successful before, like the Maintenance of Way Employees and the Railway Clerks; and at the same time water transportation rose to the class of highly organized industries, due in the main to the spectacular growth of the seamen's and longshoremen's unions.

Partly as a result of the temporary effects of industrial depression and partly the effect of the permanent liquidation of war industries, the period from 1920 to 1923 was one of falling membership. In the drop practically all labor organizations shared. Those which had been most heavily represented in the war industries and which had experienced the most substantial gains, were in the period of deflation the heaviest losers. The metal and transportation unions alone contributed about 60 per cent of the total loss in this period. The textile and packing-house unions lost about as much as they had gained. As before, the established organizations of skilled craftsmen, like the railway brotherhoods; the trade unions of skilled workers in the building trades, like the bricklayers' union; and the United Mine Workers retained what they had won. The rest of the unions appear to be in 1923 on a slightly higher level of membership than they were in the pre-war years, but they still remain much below the heights they had climbed in 1920. In the clothing industry, alone, among the industries which were weak in labor organization before the war, is unionism now on a new and higher level than that of 1914. The chemical, food, iron and steel, metal and textile industries are now, as they have been for many years, in the main poorly organized. Aggregate membership in these industries is substantial, but in proportion to the number employed in them it is slight.

Measured by the number included in its ranks, the position of the American Federation of Labor is relatively stronger at the end than at the beginning of the period, 1897–1923. In 1897, nearly 40 per cent of the total membership of American unions was claimed by labor organizations independent of the American Federation of Labor; by 1923 the membership of independents had dropped to 19 per cent of the total. This trend is attributable to the fact that the group of independent unions, composed largely of the railroad unions, has not grown by the addition of new independent organizations. Of the outstanding independent unions not in the railroad group, the bricklayers and Western Federation of Miners finally became affiliated, but the Amalgamated Clothing Workers has remained independent. New unions are generally sponsored by the Federation and naturally become affiliated with that organization from the very outset. Since it is the new and weak unions which have the greatest capacity for growth, it is not surprising that affiliated membership has grown more rapidly than that of the independent unions.

The number of women in trade unions has in the decade from 1910 to 1920 increased almost fivefold. Compared, however, with the working population of women, the number in unions is still small and in all industries women are much less organized than men. The principal cause of this condition is, of course, the fact that women work largely in occupations such as trade and domestic service, in which men are also poorly organized, and that they do not work in industries like building and mining, in which the extent of trade union organization is very great indeed. In general, it appears to be true that in industries where both men and women work, an onrush of labor organization brings both men and women into the union, but, unless membership is protected by some such device as the closed shop, the male members become relatively more numerous than the female.

The statistics of union membership, which are the basis of the conclusions just cited, are obtained either directly or indirectly from unions themselves. Although unions are in large part fighting organizations that might be expected on occasion to derive advantage from either concealing their strength or exaggerating it, their reports bear, with few exceptions, every evidence of accuracy and truthfulness. The striking losses in membership following the business recessions of 1914 and 1921 are faithfully reported by all of the unions. Wherever it was possible to check published figures of membership against the financial statements of the union, the essential accuracy of the published data was established. In a few minor instances figures reported by the union appeared to be padded and in those cases the union statistics were replaced by independent estimates. Where, also, the union refused or was unable to give any figures, as was the case with the Industrial Workers of the World and the Amalgamated Textile Workers, no data were put into the tables.

It is unfortunate for the purposes of this investigation that it was found impossible to collect monthly statistics of membership. Since business fluctuations are not synchronous in all industry, the monthly data would probably have brought to light many important correlations which are concealed in the annual statistics. A comparison, similarly, of the relation between paid-up membership and the number of members in arrears would have indicated with greater precision than do the present figures the effect of business conditions on the strength of unions. But, aside from the fact that the rules concerning lapsing of membership vary widely from union to union, such data were in no form available for publication. The figures used, then, represent annual membership. Even the annual statistics are not free of the danger of misinterpretation. Some unions report as their annual membership the average in a calendar year; others the average in a fiscal year; and still others, the membership on a specified day in each year. The resultant data, consequently, constitute a composite in which actual minor and frequent fluctuations do not appear.

Much, likewise, could have been learned from a detailed study of the geographical distribution of the membership of American labor organizations, and many attempts were made to collect the raw materials for such a study. They did not, however, meet with success. Some unions did not keep their records in such a form as to permit the geographical classification of their membership. Others, which had adequate records, were unable, because of the strategic significance of the figures, to publish them. Trial computations of the membership of local unions, based on their voting strength in the conventions of the national unions, disclosed serious discrepancies and inconsistencies and forced the rejection of such estimates. Even to a greater degree the statistics of membership of state federations of labor and of central labor councils proved fragmentary and unsatisfactory. The concentration of labor organizations in the large cities of the East and Middle West and in the coal mining areas is, of course, generally known. The essential character of the American labor movement cannot, however, be properly appreciated until its sectional distribution is accurately and fully measured.

Except for these gaps, the underlying data are reliable. The statistics of the last ten years, however, are superior in accuracy to those of the preceding period and they are constantly improving. This is due to the fact that the central offices of trade unions in the United States have had their most marked development in recent years. Unions have for many years been adding to the efficiency of their central and local offices and are improving their bookkeeping and accounting systems. The benefit-paying unions have, of course, always kept excellent records; but for the great bulk of labor organizations, the maintenance of adequate records is a practice of comparatively recent origin.

The most convenient single source for the statistics of union membership is the annual convention proceedings of the American Federation of Labor. Since 1897 each annual report of the proceedings contains a table showing the voting strength of each affiliated national or international union and of all directly affiliated local unions. According to the constitution of the Federation [1] each delegate to the annual convention can "cast one vote for every one hundred members or major fraction thereof he represents."

[1] Article IV, sec. 3.

The voting strength of a union is computed from the monthly payment of per capita tax to the American Federation of Labor.[1] The membership of each organization is, therefore, obtained by multiplying its voting strength by one hundred. In the main, figures so derived are reliable and useful. Occasionally, however, a union will pay to the Federation the per capita tax on a fixed membership, either for the purpose of concealing its real strength, to save money, or as a matter of convenience alone.[2] For these reasons the statistics were obtained, wherever possible, from the records of the unions. In the remaining cases the figures used were those published in the proceedings of the Federation.

Fluctuations in the membership of the American Federation of Labor do not, however, satisfactorily reflect changes in the membership of the total labor movement. As at present constituted and almost throughout its whole history, the American labor movement has been composed of many diverse elements. There were for example in 1923, 108 national and international unions affiliated with the American Federation of Labor. Not all of these organizations have been continuously affiliated with the Federation. The bricklayers' union became affiliated only a few years ago; the Western Federation of Miners remained independent for a long period and finally for a few years became an affiliated organization. As existing unions are added or dropped from the roster of the Federation, the membership of that organization would show changes not representative of the variations in the total membership of trade unions. In addition to such unions as these, which have had a changing relationship with the American Federation of Labor, there are a group of large national unions, like the railroad brotherhoods and the Amalgamated Clothing Workers, which have always been independent of the Federation. The membership of such unions does not, of course, appear in the Federation proceedings but it is included in the tables of this study. Scattered over the

[1] Article IV, sec. 4.

[2] Mr. Hugh Frayne points out that in periods of depression and widespread unemployment many unions will pay per capita taxes to the American Federation of Labor only on their dues-paying membership, while they retain on their books a substantial number of bona fide members who have, because of unemployment, fallen in arrears. Where this is the case, the membership statistics of the American Federation of Labor underestimate the effective membership of its affiliated organizations. This condition no doubt accounts for a portion of the drop in membership since 1920.

country are a substantial number of independent local unions affiliated neither with the American Federation of Labor nor with the independent national organizations. Important unions of this type, like the Tapestry Carpet Workers, the Mechanical Workers' Union of Amsterdam, N. Y., and others, play a considerable part in the labor movement in the textile industry. To collect the statistics of membership of these organizations, even for a single year, would involve the taking of a census at a considerable expense, not justified by the results. They are, consequently, here omitted.[1]

The omission of independent local unions and of a few national unions, which refuse to publish their membership, leads to a slight underestimate in total membership. This is partly compensated for by an overestimate in the membership of local unions directly affiliated with the American Federation of Labor. Directly affiliated local unions are organized by the Federation in industries and localities where there is no existing national union or where the national union is weak. As they grow in number and extent they are frequently formed into national organizations. In 1923 there were 523 of such local unions in the Federation. Since many of them, which have an average annual membership of less than fifty, are allowed at least one delegate to the convention, membership computed from their voting strength is too large. With every possible allowance for this exaggeration, it is estimated that the present total membership of American trade unions is probably from 100,000 to 200,000 greater than the totals shown in the following tables.

Most American trade unions admit to membership Canadians working in the industries over which they claim jurisdiction. Since 1911 the Canadian membership of American unions is available in the annual reports of the Canadian Department of Labor. Because this Canadian membership adds directly to the financial resources and total strength of American parent organizations, it is not de-

[1] Unions independent of the American Federation of Labor are of two types. The first type consists of unions, like the railroad brotherhoods, whose jurisdictional claims do not overlap those of organizations affiliated with the American Federation of Labor. Unions of the second type, on the other hand, challenge the jurisdiction of affiliated organizations and are, therefore, regarded by the Federation as "dual" unions. Jurisdiction over men's clothing workers is, for example, claimed by the United Garment Workers and over all textile workers by the United Textile Workers. Accordingly, independent unions like the Amalgamated Clothing Workers and many small unions of textile workers are frequently described as "dual" unions.

ducted from the total membership of the American unions. But when comparison is made between the number of organized workers and the number gainfully employed in the United States, proper deduction is in each case made of the Canadian membership.

Only in a few cases do the unions keep adequate records of female membership. It was frequently necessary, therefore, to rely for the statistics of women members on the estimates of trade union officials and to limit the study of these figures to the years 1910 and 1920. The final statistics appear to be reasonably accurate; if anything they underestimate slightly, perhaps from 25,000 to 50,000, the total female membership of American labor organizations.

Much would be gained both in accuracy and in usefulness if some agency such as the United States Bureau of Labor Statistics undertook the publication of an annual or biennial report on the statistics of union membership. The unwillingness of many labor organizations to file their statistics with public bureaus, which prevailed until recently, is now a thing of the past. The requirements of frequent reporting would inevitably lead to a closer scrutiny of the materials and hence to more reliable statistical data. This is particularly true with regard to the statistics of women membership, where the periodic issue of government reports would unquestionably bring the unions to the establishment of a permanent system of bookkeeping in which male and female membership was distinguished and separately kept.

CHAPTER II

CHANGES IN UNION MEMBERSHIP, 1880–1923

The year 1897 may conveniently be chosen as the beginning of the contemporary phase of the American labor movement. By that time the struggle for supremacy between the Knights of Labor and the American Federation of Labor, begun in the early eighties, had been settled with a victory for the Federation. In the middle nineties the Knights of Labor, which had pursued so spectacular a career in the decade from 1880 to 1890, had practically disappeared from the field, to remain thereafter a shadow of its former self with only a handful of members. The independent and insurgent railroad workers' movements of the early 1890's had likewise ended, leaving the conservative railroad brotherhoods in full command of the situation. Old and new trade unions, adhering now to more conservative strike and organization policies, took measures to build stronger foundations for the future. And the serious business depression, with its concomitants of extensive business failures and vast unemployment, was about to turn into recovery.

For the purposes of statistical analysis it is essential to comprehend the nature of the labor movement in the period from 1880 to 1897. The Knights of Labor, which was for a time the dominant factor in the field, had all the characteristics of an unstable and impermanent organization. It owed its striking growth from 1884 to 1886 to participation in a wave of country-wide strikes which brought into the organization thousands of unskilled workers, hitherto unorganized and apparently not then in a position to adhere permanently to a labor organization. The machinery for consolidating these great gains the organization of the Knights lacked. The energies of its officers and members were dissipated in a great variety of coöperative and political enterprises, for the successful conduct of which the Knights had neither the financial resources nor the administrative skill. Its accessions in membership, at the height of its success, were not of the type to yield a large treasury and a disciplined and stable rank and file.

The Knights were not, moreover, in unchallenged control of the enterprise of organizing the unorganized workers of the country. For many years there had existed more or less powerful organizations of skilled workers, such as the bricklayers', printers', cigarmakers', iron molders', steel workers', and railroad workers' unions, which were drawn into the strikes of the period, without being able to dictate their strategy or to control their duration. These organizations manifested then, as they do now, a strong inclination for autonomy in the management of the affairs of the industry or occupation over which they happened to have jurisdiction. To be drawn into strikes, which they frequently considered ill-advised and for grievances which they sometimes regarded as not their own, became a source of constant irritation and of growing resentment.

In November, 1881, the Federation of Organized Trades and Labor Unions was organized in the city of Pittsburgh. This organization, the direct precursor of the American Federation of Labor, had as its principal moving spirit, Samuel Gompers. Whatever may have been the motives and intentions of its founders, the Federation became the rallying point for the unions of skilled workers, the trade unions. Before long it was involved in open conflict with the Knights of Labor. By the close of this decade, organizations affiliated with the Knights were calling strikes against those affiliated with the American Federation of Labor and vice versa. The Haymarket disaster was the beginning of the end of the Knights of Labor. For all practical purposes the struggle for supremacy was over by 1890; and the trade-autonomous labor organizations, in their confederation of unions, the American Federation of Labor, had won.

It was, however, in the activities of both the Knights of Labor and the American Federation of Labor that the foundation was laid for the organization of the many trade unions that are now an integral part of the organized labor movement in this country. The years from 1885 to 1895 were exceedingly busy ones in the founding of new labor organizations which later became the national and international trade unions of today. In a formative period like that from 1880 to 1890 the spectacular successes of the Knights of Labor were enough to fire the imagination of workingmen and to pave the way for the creation of more lasting organizations. In 1886 and 1887 alone, nineteen new national unions were formed.[1]

Statistics of membership during such a period must naturally be severely discounted. Diverse cross-currents in the labor movement were simultaneously in operation, workingmen at the same time held membership in more than one of the competing unions, and joining a union was often only a temporary incident in the conduct of a strike. Such were the characteristics of the fifteen years after 1880. Warring organizations, also, with the smell of blood still fresh in their nostrils were not beyond making claims for their fighting strength, which it would be impossible now to substantiate. Nor were the records of unions, except in a few instances, in such shape as to constitute the source of adequate and reliable data. Such figures for the period as can be used should for these reasons do no more than give an impression of the general order of magnitude of the labor movement in the eighties and early nineties.

The following table is by no means complete. It does show, however, the reported membership of the Knights of Labor and the American Federation of Labor and of a number of the more important trade unions, in existence at that time. The most significant item in the table is the evidence of the very rapid recession in membership experienced by the Knights of Labor after 1886. Its imposing numbers, even if all allowance is made for inflation, it held for little more than two years. At its peak the gross membership in this decade of all American labor organizations probably did not exceed 1,000,000 and of this number, as has been said before, at least 250,000 represented a strike membership decidedly ephemeral in character.

[1] In 1886 the following national trade unions were formed: the National Union of Brewery Workers; the Metal Polishers', Buffers', Platers' and Brass Workers' International Union; the Order of Railroad Telegraphers; the Machinists' National League; the National League of Musicians; the International Musical Union; the Protective Fraternity of Printers; the Tailors' Progressive Union; the Mutual Association of Railroad Switchmen of North America; the Glass Blowers of North America; in 1887: the Brotherhood of Painters and Decorators; the Horse Collar Makers' National Union; the Building Laborers' National Union; the Saddle and Harness Makers' National Association; the Silk Workers' National Union; the Umbrella, Pipe and Cane Workers' National Union; the Paving Cutters' National Union; the Pattern Makers' League; the Brotherhood of Section Foremen. Commons and Associates, *History of Labor in the United States*, Vol. II, p. 396.

TABLE 1. — MEMBERSHIP OF SELECTED AMERICAN LABOR UNIONS, 1880–1896

Year	Knights of Labor[a]	A. F. of L.[b]	Iron Molders[c]	Brick-layers[d]	Cigar-makers[e]	Railway Conductors[f]	Typo-graphical[g]	Locomotive Firemen[h]	Railroad Trainmen[i]	Car-penters[j]	Steel Workers[k]
1880	28,136	.....	.....	.....	.....	1,050	6,520	.....	.....	.....	9,550
1881	19,422	40,000	.....	2,500	.....	1,420	7,931	3,160	.....	2,042	10,359
1882	42,517	65,000	10,000	.....	11,430	2,014	10,439	5,125	.....	3,780	16,003
1883	51,914	76,000	.....	.....	13,214	3,298	12,273	7,888	.....	3,293	11,800
1884	60,811	105,000	.....	.....	11,871	6,109	16,030	12,246	901	4,364	9,242
1885	104,066	125,000	......	7,000	12,000	7,944	16,183	14,694	4,766	5,789	5,702
1886	702,924	138,000	13,000	.....	24,672	10,330	18,484	16,196	7,993	21,423	7,219
1887	510,351	160,000	.....	.....	20,566	11,947	19,190	17,047	8,662	25,466	11,426
1888	259,578	175,000	16,000	.....	17,199	13,224	17,491	18,278	11,413	28,416	14,946
1889	220,607	210,000	.....	.....	17,555	13,720	21,120	17,087	.....	31,494	16,117
1890	100,000	225,000	23,000	24,000	24,624	14,453	22,608	18,657	13,562	53,769	20,781
1891	......	238,000	.....	.....	24,221	17,906	25,165	22,460	20,409	56,937	24,068
1892	......	255,000	.....	.....	26,678	20,224	28,187	25,967	28,540	51,313	20,975
1893	74,635	260,000	.....	.....	26,788	20,356	30,454	28,681	22,359	54,121	13,613
1894	......	275,000	.....	.....	27,828	19,827	31,379	26,508	.....	33,917	10,000
1895	......	270,000	20,000	19,500	27,760	19,737	29,295	21,408	......	25,152	10,000
1896	......	265,000	.....	.....	27,318	19,810	28,838	22,461	22,326	29,691	11,000

[a] Commons and Associates, *History of Labor in the United States*, Vol. II, pp. 339, 343–4, 381, 413, 482, 494.
[b] Estimated by reading from bar chart in annual convention proceedings.
[c] Frank T. Stockton, "The International Molders' Union of North America," *Johns Hopkins Studies*, p. 23.
[d] *Report of Officers*, 1911, p. 534.
[e] Report of President Perkins to 22d Annual Convention, 1920.
[f] E. C. Robbins, *The Railway Conductors, A Study in Organized Labor*.
[g] G. E. Barnett, *The Printers, A Study in American Trade Unionism*, p. 375.
[h] *Brotherhood of Locomotive Firemen and Enginemen's Magazine*, May, 1922.
[i] D. L. Cease, "Brotherhood of Railroad Trainmen," in *Gunton's Magazine*, March, 1901.
[j] *Convention Proceedings*, 1916, p. 77.
[k] J. S. Robinson, "The Amalgamated Association of Iron, Steel and Tin Workers," *Johns Hopkins Studies*, 1920, p. 21.

Beginning, roughly, in 1897 the American labor movement thereafter pursued a steadier and apparently a more permanent course. In the last twenty-seven years trade union membership has experienced marked growth. In 1923 membership was roughly 3,330,000 greater than at the beginning of the period and a little more than a million greater than at the beginning of the World War. As the next two tables indicate, except for the large recession since 1920,

TABLE 2. — TOTAL MEMBERSHIP OF AMERICAN TRADE UNIONS 1897–1923

Year	Membership	Year	Membership	Year	Membership
1897	447,000	1906	1,958,700	1915	2,607,700
1898	500,700	1907	2,122,800	1916	2,808,000
1899	611,000	1908	2,130,600	1917	3,104,600
1900	868,500	1909	2,047,400	1918	3,508,400
1901	1,124,700	1910	2,184,200	1919	4,169,100
1902	1,375,900	1911	2,382,800	1920	5,110,800
1903	1,913,900	1912	2,483,500	1921	4,815,000
1904	2,072,700	1913	2,753,400	1922	4,059,400
1905	2,022,300	1914	2,716,900	1923	3,780,000

this growth was a steady and almost continuous one. Losses in membership were in each case associated with and were probably, in part at least, the effect of business depression. Thus the periods of loss in membership, 1904–1906, 1908–1909, 1913–1915, and 1920–1923, correspond roughly with the periods of business decline. There is no question that monthly statistics of membership would show even closer correspondence. Except, also, for the year 1923 and possibly 1922, the years of business revival are generally those of gain in membership. Except again for the period, 1920–1923, which presents peculiarities and the result of which is still uncertain, the recessions of the past were more than made up by subsequent rises in membership.

The detailed data of the membership of all trade unions, from 1897 to 1923, are shown in Table I.[1] In this table the unions are classified in the groups used by Professor Barnett in his two articles. While some unions, like the United Brotherhood of Carpenters, which includes in its membership factory woodworkers as well as outside carpenters, properly fall into several classes, no attempt

[1] Appendix. All tables designated by Roman numbers are in the Appendix.

was made to distribute the membership of any union among the various groups. The Maintenance of Way Employees were unwilling to submit their membership for the years 1920, 1921, and 1922. Since the figures for 1919 and 1923 were available, the estimates in the table were derived by simple interpolation on the assumption that there was in the period a gradual drop in membership. This assumption is not far from the truth. The Amalgamated Textile Workers were likewise reluctant to give any figures for the years after 1920. In this case no reasonable basis for estimate

TABLE 3. — CHANGES IN TOTAL MEMBERSHIP
1897–1923

Period	Gain or Loss in Membership			
	Number		Per Cent	
	In period	Average per year	In period	Average per year
1897–1904	+ 1,625,700	+ 232,243	+ 363.7	+ 52.0
1904–1906	− 114,000	− 57,000	− 5.5	− 2.8
1906–1908	+ 171,900	+ 85,950	+ 8.8	+ 4.4
1908–1909	− 83,200	− 83,200	− 3.9	− 3.9
1909–1913	+ 706,000	+ 176,500	+ 34.5	+ 8.6
1913–1915	− 145,700	− 72,850	− 5.3	− 2.6
1915–1920	+ 2,503,100	+ 500,620	+ 96.0	+ 19.2
1920–1923	− 1,330,800	− 443,600	− 26.0	− 8.7
1897–1923	+ 3,333,000	+ 123,444	+ 745.6	+ 27.6

could be found. It is known, however, that this organization lost heavily in membership in the past three years. The net effect of this omission is to underestimate the recent membership of the textile group and to exaggerate somewhat, but not greatly, the degree of the fall since 1920.

Changes in total membership over the period were not shared alike or at the same time by the component unions. The time and extent of recession and of recovery varied widely among the groups and among particular organizations. Practically all of the groups participated in the steady growth that began in 1897, when the majority of the unions were small and just getting on their feet, and was interrupted by the decline in business of 1903–1904. Only two important groups of unions moved up and down within this period, the mining and quarrying, and textile groups. Both have been subject to violent and frequent fluctuations in membership throughout their history. While the progress of the coal union, the largest union in the mining and quarrying group, has been steadily upward, it has experienced in its conflicts with coal operators many vicissitudes, it has engaged in frequent strikes, and has often launched vigorous organization campaigns in both the anthracite and bituminous districts which have alternately failed and succeeded. These engagements have resulted in accessions and losses in membership, more frequent than those of unions which have had a more quiet development. The important textile unions have been and are notoriously weak. Their industrial relations, like those of the miners, have often been dotted with great strikes and organization campaigns that have meant a fluctuating membership.

The steadiest growth is found in the three important groups of building, transportation and printing unions. In all of these groups, the dominant organizations are the old and well-established unions which were operating with considerable force even before 1897. After the first phase of rapid growth, terminating somewhere between 1904 and 1905, these unions were only slightly affected by the business recessions prior to that of 1920. Unions in the building trades dropped 4.8 per cent in 1904, 4.2 per cent in 1908 and 3.7 per cent from 1913 to 1915. The printing unions lost 7 per cent from 1904 to 1907, 4.5 per cent in 1908 and had no losses again until 1921. Similarly the transportation group had an unbroken rise from 1909 to 1920, but fell 5.6 per cent in 1905 and 6.8 per cent in 1908. Two other groups, still relatively a small part of the total membership of American trade unions, had the longest periods of uninterrupted increase. The early rise in the membership of the musical and theatrical unions is due wholly to the steady growth of the musicians' unions and of the theatrical stage employees' organization; while the increase in the membership of the public service group is a function almost entirely of the growth of the letter carriers' and post-office clerks' unions, both of which had in 1900 a membership of only 15,400.

Conditions affecting the growth of trade unions in the years 1915 to 1923 are of particular interest. In this period were felt the effects of the war, of the post-war boom, and of the subsequent depression lasting from 1920 to 1922. It is clear that, during this whole time, the labor movement worked under circumstances not likely to be soon duplicated. Because of heavy foreign purchasing in the United States, the depression of 1914 was converted rapidly into intense business activity. The European conflict made greater and greater demands on American industry and agriculture. With the entry of the United States into the war in April, 1917, our war requirements led to the development on a vast scale of so-called war industries, produced some diversion from civilian to war industry production, and left the output of strictly non-war goods at its previously high level.

Accustomed to draw a large part of its increments of labor from the immigrant labor market, this country met these extraordinary new demands for additional production with the supply of immigrant labor practically cut off by the various war blockades. The cessation of this influx of immigrants, which before the war had amounted to almost 1,000,000 a year, was bound to produce amid conditions of intense business activity a stringent labor market, full employment and rising wages. These results, already apparent before the beginning of 1917, became more manifest after the American declaration of war.

The urgent need for uninterrupted production and the fear that competitive bidding for labor, high labor mobility and threatened strikes would impede the war program led to the swift adoption of schemes of government controls over industry and to the active participation by the government in the processes of collective bargaining and industrial relations. Government labor boards were set up in the transportation, clothing, shipbuilding, leather and other industries. On these boards the representatives of organized workingmen had both a seat and a voice. Impending disputes were in many cases resolved by submission for settlement to the representatives of trade unions, who in this manner gained in prestige and influence.

All of these factors, naturally, were highly favorable to the spread of labor organization. The slackening of immigration and the activity of business produced a rising labor market. A high level of employment among factory workers is a condition peculiarly favorable to the vigorous and successful conduct of campaigns of organization. Workers then do not fear discharge and they are generally anxious to avail themselves of their collective bargaining power and of the skill of trade union officials in winning concessions in wages, hours and working conditions. Furthermore, to a greater degree than at any time before, unions were operating more or less under the ægis of the government. The result was a continuous and substantial rise in membership.

These conditions of business prosperity and of a tight labor market did not end with the signing of the armistice in the fall of 1918. There was, to be sure, a period of lull in business and industry lasting some three or four months. But after the first quarter of 1919 industrial activity increased again and prices and wages rose to new high levels. The fresh revival and boom continued into 1920 when it stopped short in the early months of that year, first in one industry and then in another. By the middle of the year some industries were already in a deep slump which soon spread over industry in general. During 1921 the volume of unemployment was large and wages were falling.

Revival set in once more in the last half of 1922. Prices began slowly to rise; industrial operations were resumed; and at the beginning of 1923 business and industry were again in full swing. While a perceptible slackening took place in April or May of 1923, that year as a whole is now generally regarded as a prosperous one. In it there was full employment, rising prices and wages, and a high level of business earnings.

To all of these changes in business and to other pertinent factors, union membership reacted promptly and perceptibly. From 1915 to 1920 labor organizations gained 2,503,100 members, a gain almost as great as their total membership in 1914. Again, in the next three-year period, more than one-half of this gain, or 1,330,800 members, were lost. Industrial depression and revival do not strike all industries at the same time or to the same degree. Various groups of unions, consequently, may be expected to show marked variation in the rise and fall of their membership. The broad facts concerning these differences are shown in the following table.

TABLE 4.—PER CENT OF GAIN OR LOSS IN MEMBERSHIP 1915–1923

Group of Unions	1915–1920	1920–1921	1921–1922	1922–1923
Mining	+ 25.7	+ 6.5	– 14.5	+ 9.2
Building	+ 66.7	– 2.1	– 4.9	+ 2.2
Metal	+ 283.1	– 15.2	– 30.5	– 29.1
Textile	+ 565.6	– 40.9	– 58.1	+ 1.6
Clothing	+ 113.2	– 12.1	– 4.1	+ 1.0
Leather	+ 113.8	– 14.7	– 6.2	– 18.9
Transportation	+ 118.1	– 1.3	– 16.2	– 8.7
Paper	+ 41.9	+ 10.7	– 11.6	– 5.8
Lumber	+ 15.6	– 17.6	– 38.8	– 13.9
Chemical	– 2.6	+ 2.7	– 6.4	– 8.8
Food	+ 4.0	– 1.6	– 18.1	– 7.4
Restaurant	+ 75.4	– 16.5	– 32.3	– 28.6
Theatre	+ 13.7	+ 7.5	+ 1.1	+ 0.3
Public Service	+ 78.3	+ 6.4	– 0.6	+ 0.9
Total	+ 96.0	– 5.8	– 15.7	– 6.9

Among the more important groups of unions, obviously, the most striking growth in membership from 1915 to 1920 was made by the textile, metal, transportation, clothing, leather and building groups. The great rise in textile membership is not so significant as it seems, because the base is so low, its membership in 1915 being only 22,400. The rise in the other groups, however, is large in either absolute or relative terms. The total rise in the membership of the building trades unions should not properly be credited to the construction industry alone, since, as it has already been said, unions like the carpenters, electrical workers and painters have a substantial membership outside of the building industry. Many members, likewise, of the metal trades unions worked in railroad shops and would have contributed appreciably, if materials for distributing the statistics had been available, to the increase in membership of the transportation group.

Some of the groups which contributed most heavily to the rise were most severely hit in the subsequent drop in membership. Thus both the metal and textile groups suffered uniformly large losses in each of the three years from 1920 to 1923. The transportation group also incurred substantial losses. The large variations in the degree of loss in each of the years from 1920 to 1923 are probably more apparent than real and are at least partly due as much to defects in the statistics as to fact. In the first place, practice among unions varies with regard to their treatment of members who fail to pay dues. Keeping large numbers of such members on the rolls of the union will produce a considerable lag between a drop in business and a fall in union membership. Secondly, a great many unions submit their membership statistics in the form of the average membership for the fiscal year ending somewhere toward the middle of that year. In this case, the prevailing method of reporting probably underestimates the magnitude of the fall from 1920 to 1921 and exaggerates it from 1921 to 1922. On the other hand, it is no doubt true that there is actually a considerable lag between the incidence of unemployment and the surrender of union membership. In any event, the data in the table indicate a slackening in the rate of fall in membership during the past year. Thus a loss from 1920 to 1921 of 295,800 members rose to 755,600 in 1921 to 1922 and fell to 279,400 in the last year of the period. Moreover four important groups show slight increases in membership from 1922 to 1923. While the loss in total membership was 279,400, the mining, building, textile and clothing groups gained; the mining group substantially and the rest only slightly.

Although the great rise from 1915 to 1920 and the severe decline in the next years was shared by all of the important groups of unions, there is no question that the unions claiming jurisdiction over industries most directly affected by the war felt both the rise and fall most sharply. As the next table indicates, almost three-fourths of the whole gain in membership after 1915 was made in industries that experienced large expansion during the war and that were subject to some form of public control. When, however, the drop came, the largest losers both absolutely and relatively were the transportation and metal groups, which together were responsible for more than 60 per cent of the total loss of 1,330,800 members in that period. The metal unions, accordingly, lost almost five-sixths and the transportation unions nearly one-half of their previous gains. The building and clothing unions, on the other hand, suffered substantial but proportionately much smaller declines.

Gain in Total Membership, 1915–1920	2,503,100
Gain in following groups:	
Transportation	680,000
Metal	634,600
Building	355,200
Clothing	192,400
Total for above groups	1,862,200
Loss in Total Membership, 1920–1923	1,330,800
Loss in following groups:	
Transportation	307,800
Metal	500,500
Building	43,500
Clothing	54,000
Total for above groups	905,800

The explanation for this concentrated loss in membership is certainly not a simple one and cannot be made in terms of business depression alone. Many and diverse factors helped to shape the course of trade union membership between the collapse of the post-war boom and the recovery of 1922–1923. The business history of the building industry differed widely from that of almost all other industries after 1920. Extensive war restrictions on private building construction resulted after 1920 in an early resumption of activity in the building industry and finally, even before the general industrial revival had begun, in an imposing building boom which has not yet altogether ended. This prolonged period of intense activity was accompanied, particularly in the larger cities, by a shortage of skilled building trades workers and consequently by a rise in the membership of the building unions. The clothing unions which encountered severe business depressions in their industry in 1921, 1922 and again in the last half of 1923, kept their losses down by prosecuting extensive organization campaigns and by engaging in strikes which for the most part were successful enough to enable them to hold the bulk of their membership.

In the steam transportation industry the efforts to retain the strength of the unions by challenging the employers in strike were equally vigorous but not so successful. The net effect of the shopmen's strike was the loss of control over many railroads and severe decreases in the membership of the machinists', railway carmen's, boilermakers', blacksmiths' and sheet-metal workers' unions. Water transportation unions, like the longshoremen, and other organizations, like the teamsters, lost heavily in membership through sheer weakness in tests of strength with the employers. Resistance, in all of these groups, to demands for wage concessions and revisions in working rules culminated in strikes which left the unions smaller than they were before.

The puzzling problem in this whole period of business recession turns on the extent of the permanent readjustment in industry that attended the liquidation of the purely war industries. The evidence on this matter is naturally not entirely convincing, but it is sufficient to permit some generalization. The year 1921 probably differs from the years of ordinary depression in business in that some of the losses in industry were more or less permanent or long-

TABLE 5.—DECREASE IN NUMBER OF WAGE EARNERS IN SELECTED GROUP OF INDUSTRIES
1919–1921

Industry	Average Number of Wage Earners		Per Cent Change
	1919	1921	
Metal, Machine Products, Shipbuilding[a]	1,903,797	1,158,657	– 39.1
Lumber	610,346	474,875	– 22.2
Printing and Publishing	287,278	268,081	– 6.6
Rubber Goods	158,549	103,273	– 34.9
Leather and Products	349,362	280,071	– 19.8
Clay, Glass, Cement Products	219,298	188,541	– 14.0
Wearing Apparel	975,780	884,035	– 9.4
Textile[b]	942,610	899,969	– 4.5
Slaughtering and Meat Packing	160,996	117,042	– 27.3
Smelting and Refining (non-ferrous)	39,620	19,014	– 52.0
Total	5,647,636	4,393,558	– 22.2

[a] Includes the following industries: farm equipment, ship and boat building, textile machinery, machine tools, typewriters, steam and electric railroad cars, railroad repair shops, electrical machinery, cast iron pipe, carriages and wagons, brass, bronze, copper and allied products, ammunitions and firearms, motor vehicles, motorcycles and bicycles, engines, locomotives and aircraft.

[b] Includes cotton manufactures, knit goods, silk manufactures, wool manufactures

time in character. This was unquestionably the case with such industries as shipbuilding and machine shops, which were either direct or auxiliary war industries and which had, therefore, abnormal expansion during the war. The preceding table, compiled from the bulletins of the 1921 U. S. Census of Manufactures, shows the drop in the number of wage earners from 1919 to 1921 for a selected group of industries. All of them together had an average factory working force in 1921 almost one-fourth less than in 1919. But the most striking drop took place in the metal, machinery and shipbuilding group, where there was at the same time the heaviest fall in trade union membership. Within this group, moreover, those industries, in which some of the metal unions had previously made their most substantial gains, dropped even more heavily. The ship and boat building industry had in 1921, 280,000 less wage earners than in 1919, or a decrease of 72.5 per cent [1]; the machine tool industry fell 30,000 or 59.9 per cent; and the engine, locomotive and aircraft industry more than 40,000, or 54.2 per cent. It is, of course, not feasible to correlate directly these contractions in

[1] The following table, taken from Douglas and Wolfe, "Labor Administration in the Shipbuilding Industry During War Time" (*Journal of Political Economy*, Vol. XXVII, 1919) shows how entirely the increase in the number of employees in shipbuilding was a war phenomenon:

Month	Total Employees in Shipyards on Emergency Fleet Corporation Work
1917	
October	88,000 (est.)
November	120,000 (est.)
December	146,000 (est.)
1918	
January	191,000
February	204,000
March	228,000
April	258,000
May	281,000
June	314,000
July	332,000
August	352,000
September	371,000
October	375,000
November	385,000

industry with the decreases in membership of specific labor organizations, without identifying the individual members who in these years forfeited their membership. Such identification is plainly impossible. Common knowledge on the matter, however, indicates that unions like the machinists and the boilermakers and iron shipbuilders lost markedly in precisely the failing industries.

No interpretation of the course of trade union membership after 1920 can be complete without some hypothesis regarding the relative levels of industrial capacity in this country at the peak in 1920 and in the years following. It may indeed be that the war and post-war expansions brought temporarily into industry large numbers of persons who gradually left with the collapse of business and did not, for the most part, return again. This certainly happened, probably on a large scale, in the shipbuilding industry where revival did not make up for the losses in depression. Unfortunately the data of the U. S. Census of Manufactures for 1923 are not yet available in sufficient number to permit a detailed comparison of the average numbers of wage earners employed in selected

TABLE 6. — GENERAL INDEX OF EMPLOYMENT IN MANUFACTURING INDUSTRIES[a]
1920–1923

Month	1920	1921	1922	1923
January	116	77	87	98
February	115	83	88	100
March	117	84	84	102
April	117	84	83	102
May	117	85	85	102
June	118	85	87	102
July	110	85	87	100
August	110	86	88	100
September	107	87	91	100
October	103	89	93	99
November	97	89	94	99
December	91	90	97	97

[a] *Monthly Labor Review,* U. S. Department of Labor, July, 1924, p. 153.

industries in 1921 and 1923. What statistical straws there are indicate that the pay rolls of manufacturing industries were uniformly lower, with reference to the numbers employed in 1923, also regarded as a year of prosperity, than in the year 1920. Thus the accompanying table on average monthly employment from 1920 to 1923 shows that average numbers of persons on the pay rolls of manufacturing industries in the United States in 1920 were 10 per cent greater than in 1923; and that the peak numbers were almost 15 per cent greater in 1920 than in the later year. The same general conclusions are supported by similar data on fluctuations in employment in New York State, collected by the office of the New York Industrial Commissioner. In that state the number on factory pay rolls was roughly 7 per cent greater in 1920 than in 1923; and the peak number in the earlier year was about 10 per cent higher than in the later year. So far as these figures have any meaning at all they would seem to indicate a general contraction in manufacturing industry in the United States since 1920, which reflects itself in the widespread and appreciable employment of fewer persons. It is unfortunate that the available statistics still throw but little light on the nature of the absorption of this excess industrial population that must have taken place in these years. But it would seem to be reasonably clear that such a contraction did occur and that it accounts, in part at least, for the precipitate drop in the membership of labor organizations from the peak of business in 1920 to the next year of business prosperity, 1923.

In general, old established labor organizations are less subject to marked fluctuations in their membership than recently organized and weak unions. Whether the general movement is upward or downward, the strong unions as a rule contribute relatively less to the total gains or losses. This was not true, of course, in the earliest periods when the great majority of unions were all small and had just begun to organize their trades or industries. It is also not true even in the later phases, when a strong and well-established organization is forced to face the problem of holding its control over an industry that is rapidly undergoing a technical revolution. But, with this exception, the extreme and striking movements of more recent years are due almost entirely to the changes in membership either of new and young unions, or of organizations that had not yet achieved real strength. To understand the position of these types of unions in the American labor movement it is necessary to undertake a somewhat more detailed description than has yet been given of the changes in membership of the 14 groups of unions and of the most important unions within each group.

Mining and Quarrying

Union membership in this group has throughout, as the next chart shows, been dominated by the career of the United Mine Workers. In the last year the membership of the United Mine Workers constituted more than 97 per cent of the total membership of the group. For a time, roughly from 1902 to 1911, the

CHART 1

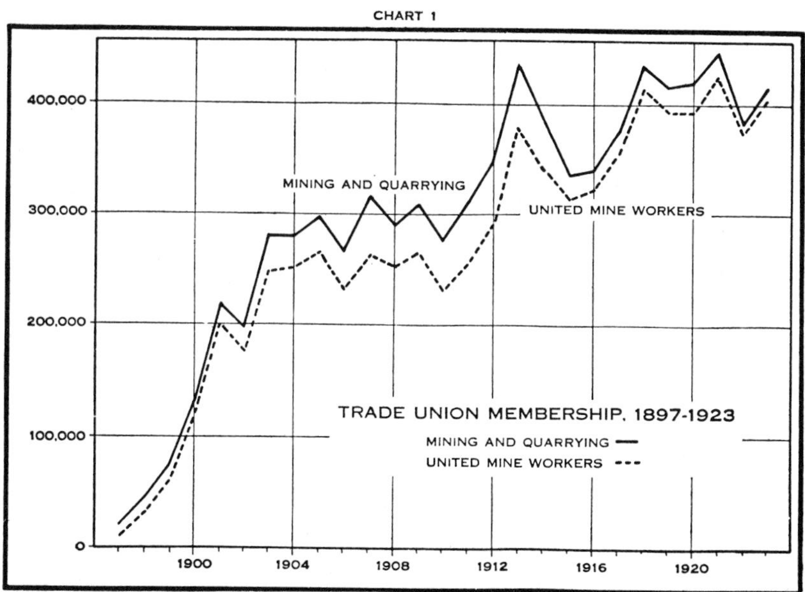

Western Federation of Miners, which claimed jurisdiction over mines other than coal, rose to a position of importance. After 1911, however, it was beaten by the employers and it has since lost consistently. Its successor, the Mine, Mill and Smelter Workers, has never achieved real strength. The statistical history of the United Mine Workers is the story of the effect on membership of a long succession of strikes and organization campaigns, which generally yielded more members. The first of the strikes, in this period, occurred in 1897. In two years membership rose more than 50,000. Both in 1900 and in 1902, the vast anthracite strikes, designed to establish the unions in the hard coal industry, terminated with the appointment of the Anthracite Coal Strike Commission, with the practical recognition of the union, and with a rise in membership from 1899 to 1905 of almost 200,000. Another anthracite strike took place in 1912 and in that same year the union was able to effect the resumption of the interstate conferences in the bituminous industry, which had for some years been suspended. From 1912 to 1913, membership rose about 90,000. The miners' union was affected during the war and post-war periods by much the same type of circumstances as influenced the growth of labor organizations in general. High levels of industrial activity and the restriction of immigration proved factors favorable to a rising membership, although the rise was interrupted in 1919 to 1920, when the union struck for wage increases in both the bituminous and anthracite fields and received from government commissions wage awards, which it regarded as unsatisfactory, and again in 1921 when it suffered the effects of severe depression in the industry. Another strike in 1922 for the purpose of organizing the non-union fields, particularly of West Virginia and Pennsylvania, and the successful issue of wage negotiations in 1923 contributed to a partial recovery from previous losses.

Building Trades

Except for the breaks due to business recessions membership in the building trades unions shows a continuous upward movement and was in 1923, 290,000 greater than in 1913. It is one of the few groups which experienced a rise after the large drop of 1920 and is also one of the few whose loss after 1920 was comparatively slight, amounting only to 6.9 per cent. The bricklayers' union, which is an old and remarkably steady organization, hardly participated at all in the general rise in membership that came after 1915. Being almost purely a building industry organization it suffered from the lull in building activity that prevailed nearly throughout the war. But for a slight rise in 1917, its membership fell until 1919, and then, stimulated by the new revival in construction, reached in 1923 a membership of 103,700, the highest point in its history. The carpenters, on the other hand, the largest union in the building trades, went up steadily until 1920 and has declined, without a break, since. This difference in the course of the membership of the bricklayers' and carpenters' unions is no doubt due to the fact that the carpenters' organization, having jurisdiction over factory workers in the lumber and other industries as well

CHART 2

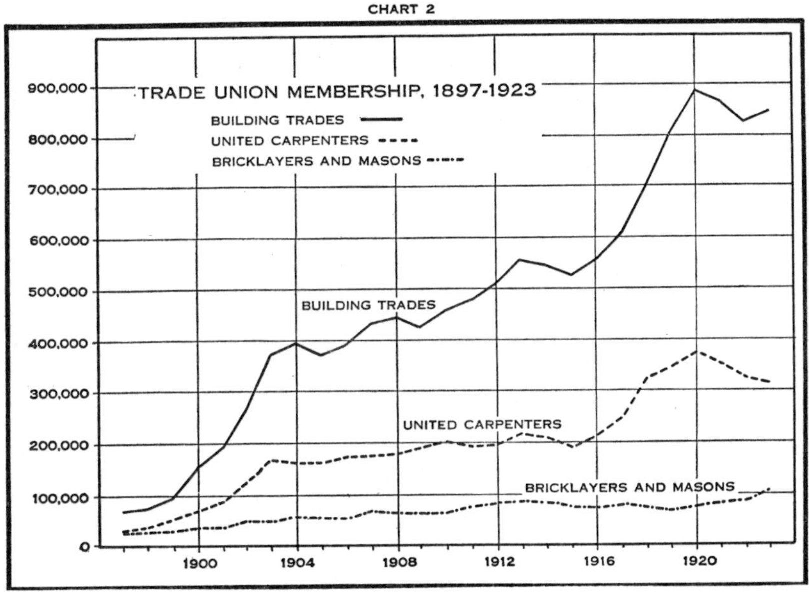

as over carpenters in the building industry, participated to a greater extent in the general rise and also in the subsequent widespread loss in membership. The carpenters' and electrical workers' unions alone were responsible for about 280,000 members out of the total gain by the building trades, from 1915 to 1920, of something more than 300,000 members. The electrical workers held their gain but the carpenters lost about 60,000 members between 1920 and 1923. In the last year, however, the carpenters were still roughly 100,000 larger than in the pre-war years.

Metal, Machinery and Shipbuilding

In this group membership after 1915 was of an entirely different order of magnitude from what it was before that period of extraordinary gain. For almost a decade prior to the war, the numbers in this group remained somewhere around 200,000, but by 1920 its membership had risen to more than 800,000, the most spectacular growth

CHART 3

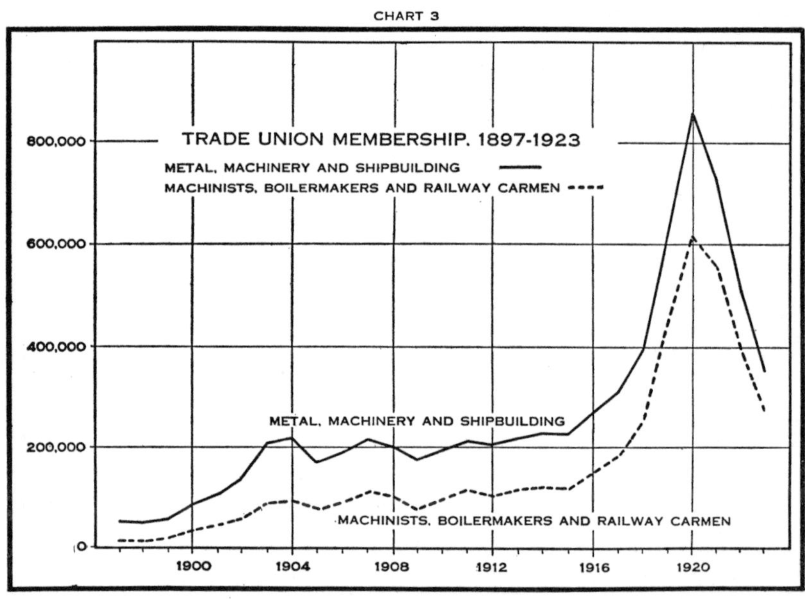

of all. This rise has already been attributed to the marked expansion of the war metal and ship industries and to the securing of a firmer foothold in the railroad shops by some unions in this group. Although this class includes a large number of organizations, substantially all of the gains and, later, the bulk of the losses were those of only a few unions: the blacksmiths, boilermakers and shipbuilders, iron, steel and tin workers, machinists and railway carmen. The machinists alone gained more than a quarter of a million members; the railway carmen, 170,000; the boilermakers over 80,000; and the blacksmiths and steel workers, smaller amounts. In the next period of loss the machinists, blacksmiths, boilermakers and steel workers suffered most heavily; the machinists alone losing more than 230,000 members. The railway carmen also declined to the extent of 40,000, but of all of the important organizations in the group, it was the most successful in preserving its war and

CHART 4

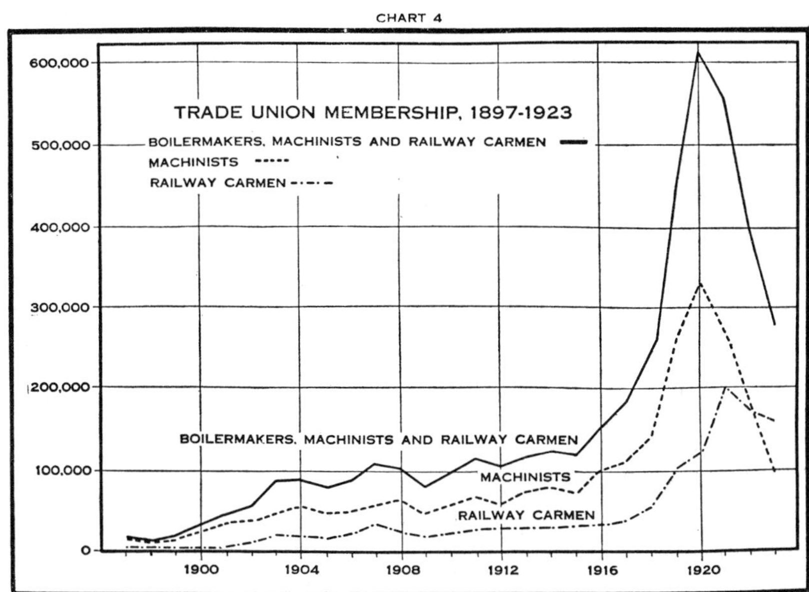

post-war gains. At the close of this period, in 1923, the membership of the railway carmen was 132,000 greater than in 1913; while the total membership of the metal group stood at, roughly, 140,000 above 1913.

Textiles

Organized labor in this group has for years been weak since there are large sections of the industry into which the unions have failed to penetrate. The large increase in membership in the years 1915–1920 of about 125,000 was due entirely to spurts in organization in which the older organization, the United Textile Workers, and the newly organized Amalgamated Textile Workers shared. Nearly all the gains were lost soon after 1920 and the whole group stood in 1923 less than 10,000 members larger than before the war. The inclusion of the figures which the Amalgamated Textile Workers refuse to give for the years 1921, 1922 and 1923 would have raised the total membership in these years little, if at all. The slight rise in membership in 1923 is due entirely to increases in the small lace operatives' and silk workers' unions. The tables on which the textile chart is based nowhere include the statistics of the membership

CHART 5

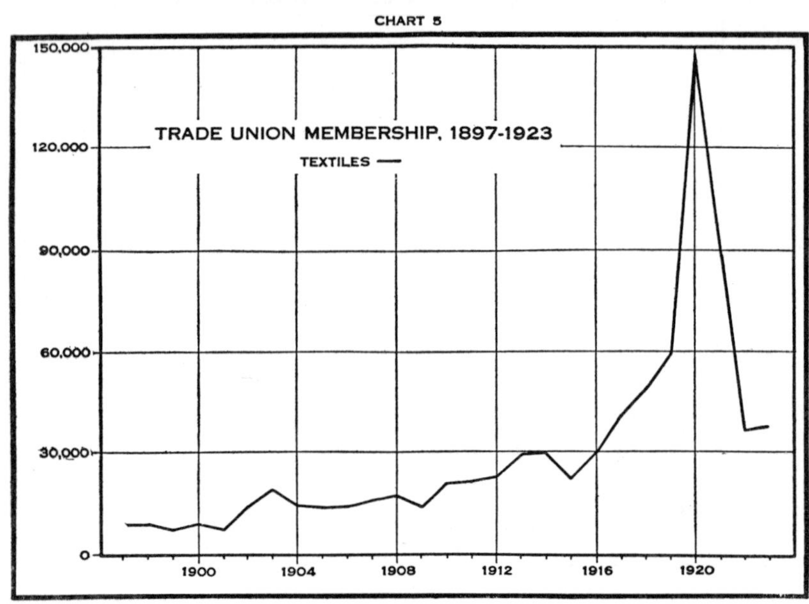

of the I. W. W. in the textile industry. It has been impossible to obtain anything but incomplete data from that organization; but it is known that the membership of both the Chicago and Detroit I. W. W.'s was less than 5,000 in 1910 and that the present organization known as the I. W. W. claimed no membership in the textile industry in 1920.

Clothing

The history of trade union membership in the clothing industry is distinguished by two important episodes; one concerned with the organization of the women's and the other with the organizaiton of the men's clothing branches of that industry. The two episodes followed one another with an interval of only a few years. Prior to 1910 there was practically no organization in the manufacture of women's clothing. The International Ladies' Garment Workers, the union claiming jurisdiction over that branch of the clothing industry, had, before 1910, a membership little larger than 2,000. In 1910 a great strike was called, which led to the rapid spread of organization and to a membership in 1911 of almost 67,000. Thereafter this union grew, except for temporary setbacks during business recessions, until it reached its peak of 105,000 in 1920.

CHART 6

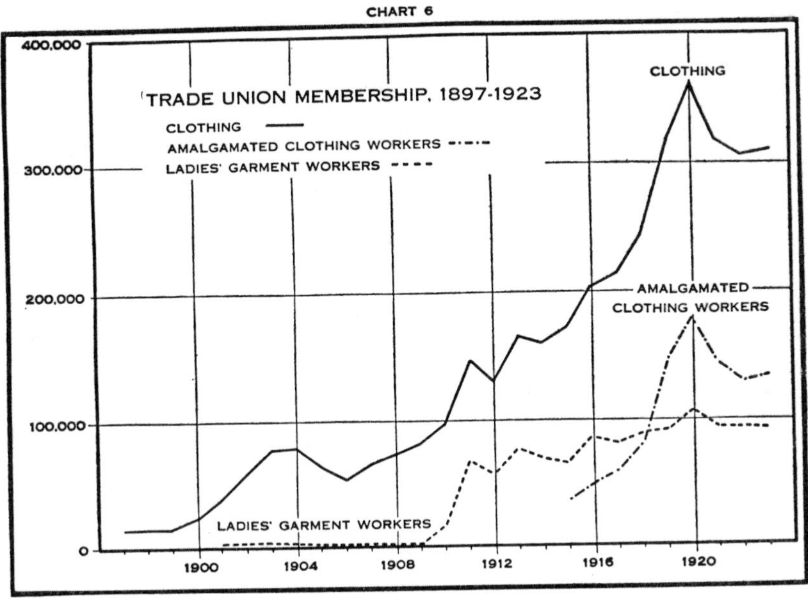

The second important incident in the history of this group came late in 1914 when the Amalgamated Clothing Workers split from the United Garment Workers and claimed jurisdiction over the men's clothing and shirt industries. While the United Garment Workers also had jurisdiction over the same industries, its membership there had always been uncertain and small, whereas it kept a fairly steady membership in the overall industry. The coming of the Amalgamated, however, brought a rapid spread of unionism in the men's clothing industry and by 1920 that union had organized the Chicago and Rochester markets, the last of the large non-union markets, and had increased the number of its members to more than 170,000. It is this increase that accounts largely for the rise in the membership of the total clothing group from 1915 to 1920. In this industry as a whole there was heavy liquidation, beginning late in 1920 and lasting for several years thereafter; and through this period both the Ladies' Garment Workers and the Amalgamated lost heavily in membership. By 1923, however, the Amalgamated showed a slight increase, whereas the movement in the women's industry was still slightly downward. The United Garment Workers and the Hatters do not appear to have been affected by the recession of business in these last years.

Leather

The course of unionism in this industry is relatively simple. After the first substantial rise in membership, in the formative

CHART 7

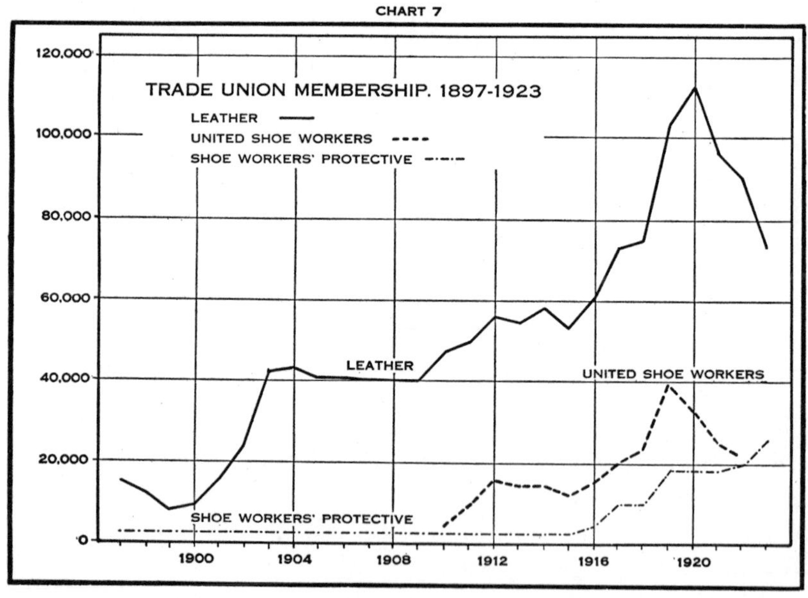

period from 1899 to 1904, the membership in this group remained practically stationary until 1910. In that year the membership of the United Shoe Workers, an independent organization which challenged the old Boot and Shoe Workers' Union for jurisdiction over the shoe industry, appeared for the first time and added substantially to the number of trade unionists in the leather group.

During the period of war expansion this organization grew somewhat more rapidly than the older union. But after 1920 all of the important unions declined, and in 1923 the United Shoe Workers' and the Shoe Workers' Protective unions were amalgamated.

Transportation

Many quite diverse elements enter into the constitution of this group. It includes such elements as the employees on steam railroads, in water transportation, teamsters and chauffeurs, workers engaged in the building of roads and streets, and the employees of street and electric railways. The movement of membership has, naturally, not been the same for all the groups, since they are

CHART 8

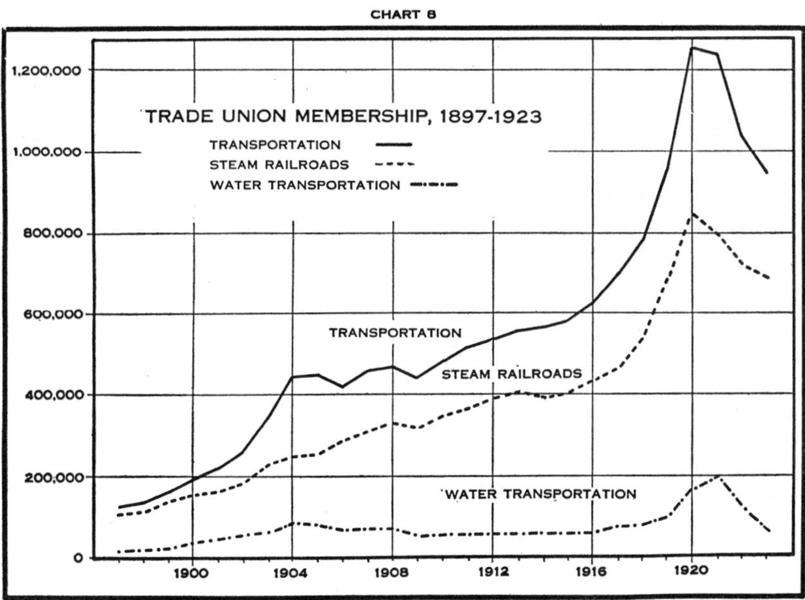

confronted by different industrial circumstances. The most striking differences are to be found in the variations in the growth of the group as a whole and of the group of unions described here as the water transportation unions. This group, composed of the longshoremen, marine engineers, masters, mates and pilots, pilots' association, and seamen, had practically a stationary membership from 1904, when its number stood at 79,800, to 1918 when it was a little above 75,000. Then for three years membership rose to the height in 1921 of over 197,000, due mainly to the great growth of the longshoremen's and seamen's unions which between them gained more than 100,000 members. Soon after there was a sudden drop, the seamen losing nearly 90,000 members, and in 1923 the membership of the group was less than it had been in 1904. Both of these large gains and losses were, in part at least, due to government intervention. The street and electric employees' union and the teamsters' organization each participated in the large rise from 1919 to 1920; the electric railway employees gaining 40,000 members and the teamsters 55,000. But in the subsequent period of general decline, the teamsters lost almost 40,000, while the electric railway employees more than held their own.

Within the steam railroad group there are, also, a variety of organizations, ranging from the stable brotherhoods, through the shop crafts, to a variegated group of organizations like the maintenance of way employees and the railway clerks. The nature of the growth and decline of organization among the shop crafts has already been discussed, so far as the available materials made it possible, in the analysis of the changes in membership in the metals group. Prior to 1917, the growth in membership of the unions on steam railroads, as is indicated in the next chart, was dominated by the changes in the membership of the four railroad brotherhoods, the locomotive engineers, locomotive firemen, railway conductors and railroad trainmen. As early as the nineties these organizations were established and their subsequent history was one of slow but steady growth. The other organizations in the industry were, however, weak and represented, in membership, but a small proportion of the whole. By 1917 the picture changed. Stimulated in large measure by the extension of government control, the formerly weak unions shot up in membership and for the period from 1917 to 1923 the two curves stand wide apart. While the increase in membership was general, the maintenance of way employees, railroad telegraphers and railway clerks contributed most of it. The maintenance of way employees rose from 5,600 in 1918 to 54,000 in 1919; the telegraphers from 27,000 in 1917 to 78,000 in 1920; and the clerks from 6,800 to 186,000 in the same period.

When the break came, all lost heavily, but they still stood in 1923 considerably above the level of 1917–1918.

The unions of the train service employees pursued a steadier and more even course. Before 1920 this group lost in membership only during the period 1913 to 1914. It reached its peak in 1919 when it had 455,700 members; fell to 425,200 in 1922; and then increased again in 1923 to 444,300.

CHART 9

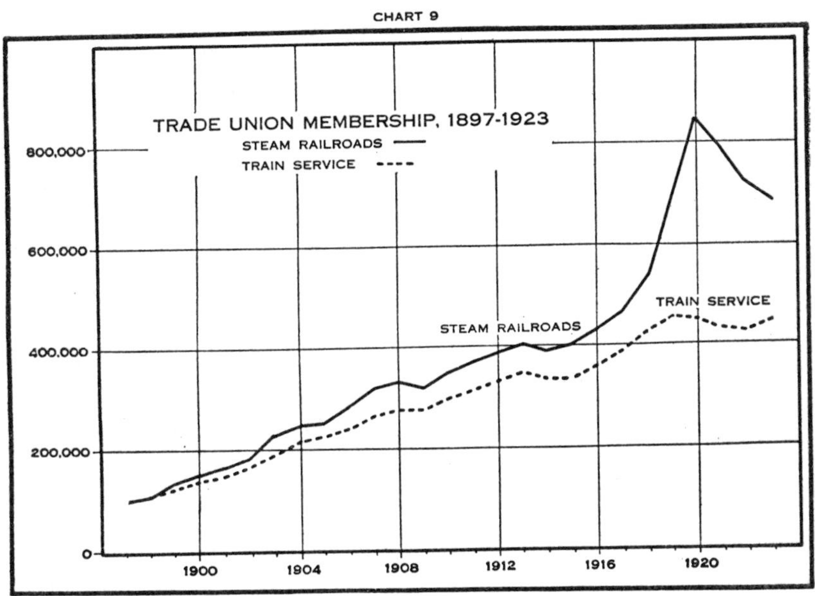

Paper, Printing and Bookbinding

While this group as a whole appears to have in 1923, even after the drop in 1921, a much larger membership than in the pre-war years, it is in reality largely the skilled printing unions that retained most of their gains. The two paper unions were in 1923 not much above their level in 1914 and 1915. The bookbinders while they gained over 16,000 from 1915 to the peak in 1921 lost nearly 12,000 in the next two years. The Typographical Union, on the other hand, although it had had a very steady and substantial growth in years before 1915, kept 9,000 members, or considerably more than half of its total rise from 1915 to the peak year, 1921; whereas at the same time the Printing Pressmen's Union added over 14,000 members and has suffered no loss since.

CHART 10

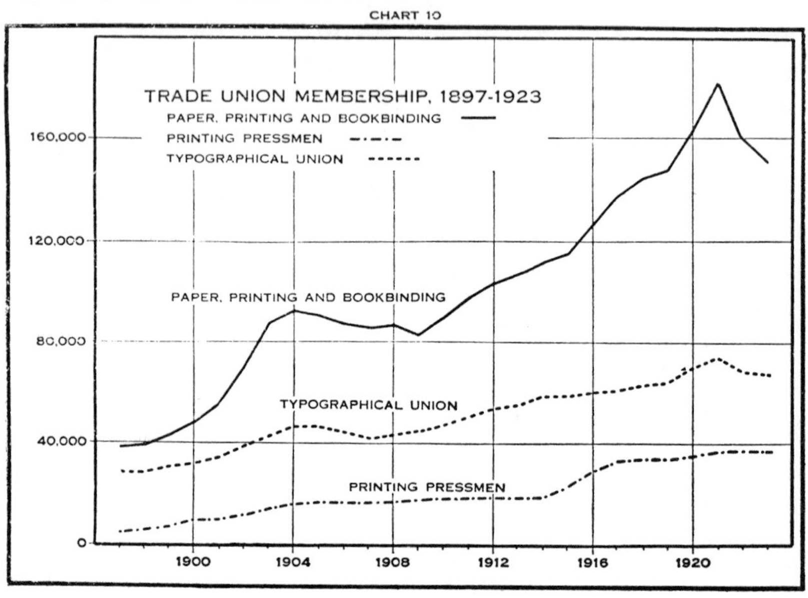

Lumber and Woodworking

Fluctuations in the membership in this group as it is now constituted are of no great significance because of the increasingly important part that the carpenters' union has come to play in the woodworking industry. The carpenters' union now not only claims jurisdiction but actually enforces its claims over "carpenter or joiner, ship-carpenter, ship-joiner, ship-caulker, shipwright, boatbuilder, railroad carpenter, bridge carpenter, dock carpenter, wharf carpenter, stair builder, floor layer, cabinet maker, bench hand, furniture worker, millwright, car-builder, boxmaker, reed and rattan worker, or engaged in the running of woodworking machinery."[1] Even as early as 1910 one-fifth of the 200,000 members of this union were employed in the lumber and woodworking industrie . The data for distributing the membership of this union in later years are not available.

[1] *Constitution*, United Brotherhood of Carpenters and Joiners, 1917.

Chemical, Clay, Glass and Stone

This is one of a few groups of labor organizations which, when their long-time history is regarded, are steadily declining, in spite of occasional but temporary revivals. The majority of the unions in this class are to be found in industries which are undergoing technical revolutions, through the introduction of machinery, as in

CHART 11

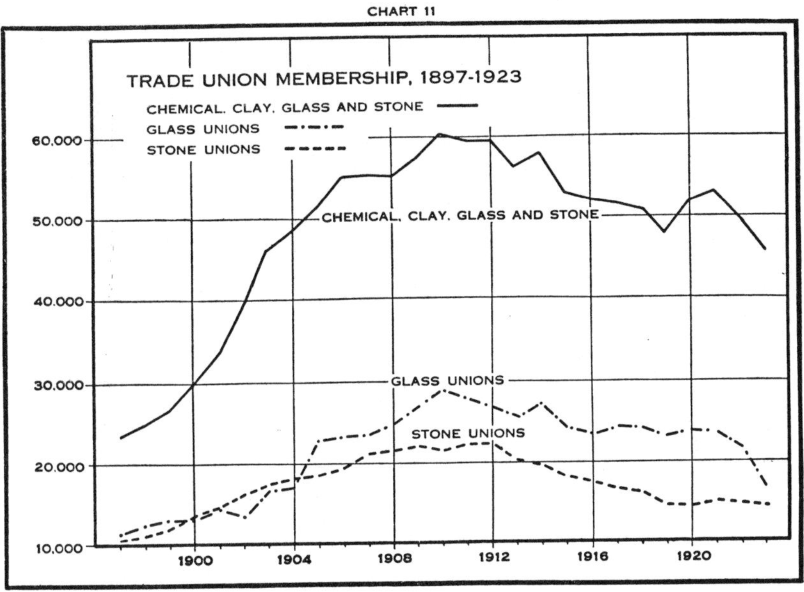

the glass industry; or whose product is in large measure being replaced by other materials, as in the stone industry. Since the middle nineties there has been a steady introduction of machinery into all branches of the glass industry; and for some years now, many new forms of building materials have replaced stone. Accordingly both the glass and stone unions show for a considerable period of years a gradual decline of membership. This decline would probably have been even more marked than it is had not a union like the Glass Bottle Blowers reported an unchanging membership of 10,000 from 1910 to 1921, when, as a matter of fact, its trend during this period was probably downward. In 1922 and 1923, however, it reports a drop first to 9,700 and then to 7,000.

Food, Liquor and Tobacco

The course of events in this group is in important respects similar to that in the preceding one. The brewery workers' union which was before prohibition one of the most powerful organizations in the country and had in 1914 a membership of more than 67,000 is now down to 16,000, although it has extended its jurisdiction claims over flour, cereal and soft drink workers. Membership statistics since 1914 for the cigarmakers' union, probably exaggerate their losses, in that they report a smaller membership to the American

CHART 12

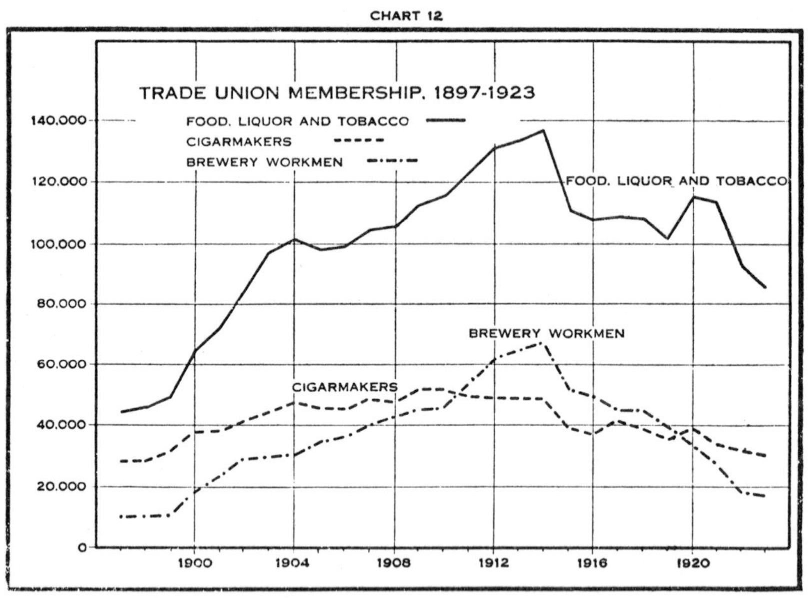

Federation of Labor than they actually have; but here, too, it is reasonably certain that the union is feeling the effects of the in-roads of machinery and new industrial processes.[1] The bakery workers' union, while it had a substantial increase during the war, has practically no membership in the large baking companies, and was never in its history successful in organizing candy workers.

[1] Report of President G. W. Perkins to 1920 Convention.

Restaurant and Trade

The important organizations in this group are the hotel workers and the meat cutters. The first union has a membership composed largely of waiters and until recently had a very solid membership among bartenders. The latter group is no longer so important. The union of meat cutters, which claims jurisdiction over slaughter and packing-house workers, conducted during the war

CHART 13

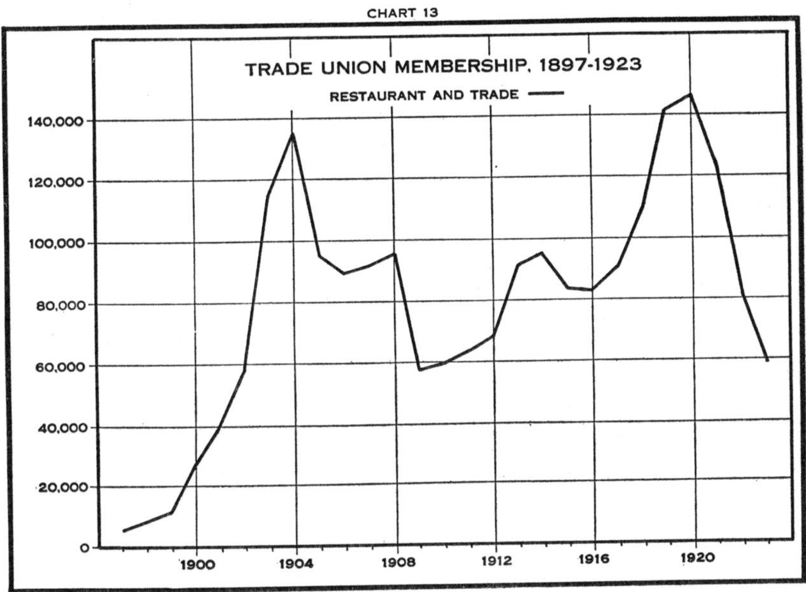

years a vigorous organization campaign in this industry and attained great strength at the peak of industrial activity in 1919 and 1920. Since then, however, it engaged in a losing strike and it has now become almost extinct in the packing industry. Organization among retail clerks, which attained before 1909 substantial proportions, has since amounted to very little.

Theatres and Music

The outstanding feature of changes in membership of the theatre and music unions is the steady growth of the musicians' and theatrical stage employees' unions, which was almost unbroken from the beginning. It is, of course, to be expected that their movement would be less affected, if at all, by the variations in business to which other types of labor organizations are so sensitive. The recession from 1914 to 1918 was due to the omission of the Musical and Theatrical Union and to a slight fall in the actors' union. The

CHART 14

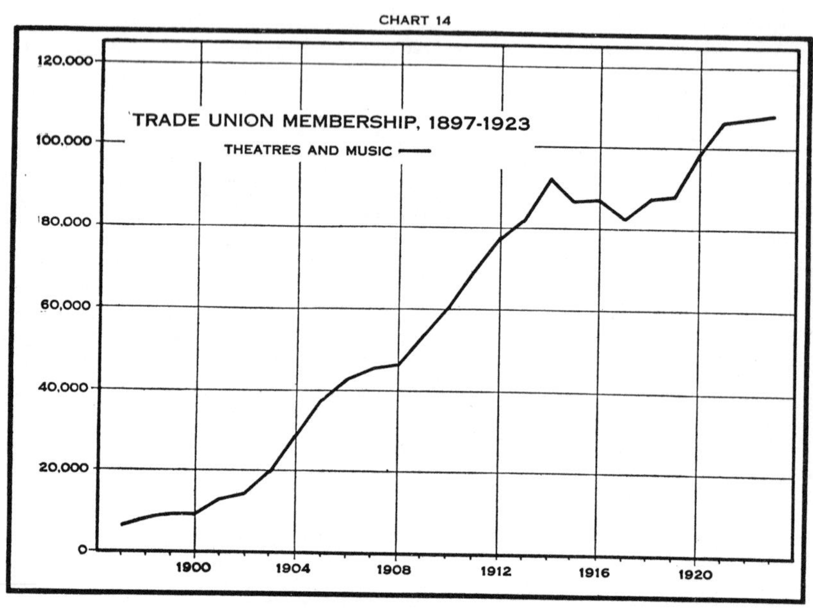

growth in membership among actors' unions is probably greater than is here indicated, since the present tables do not include all of the existing actors' organizations.

Public Service

Except for the unions of letter carriers and post-office clerks, this group is composed largely of organizations which have come into the picture within the past decade. This accounts in large measure for the striking spurt in members during the years immediately preceeding 1920, when the statistics for the federal employees', fire fighters', and teachers' unions are included for the first time in the table of membership. The losses incurred by these unions after 1920 were more than made up by the gains of the letter carriers and the two unions of post-office clerks.

Nearly half of the total membership of American unions has since 1897 been in the groups of building trades and transportation unions. The transportation unions which, at the beginning and end of the period, constitute just about one-fourth of the total membership, fell a little behind in the intervening years because of the rapid growth of unions in the building and mining

CHART 15

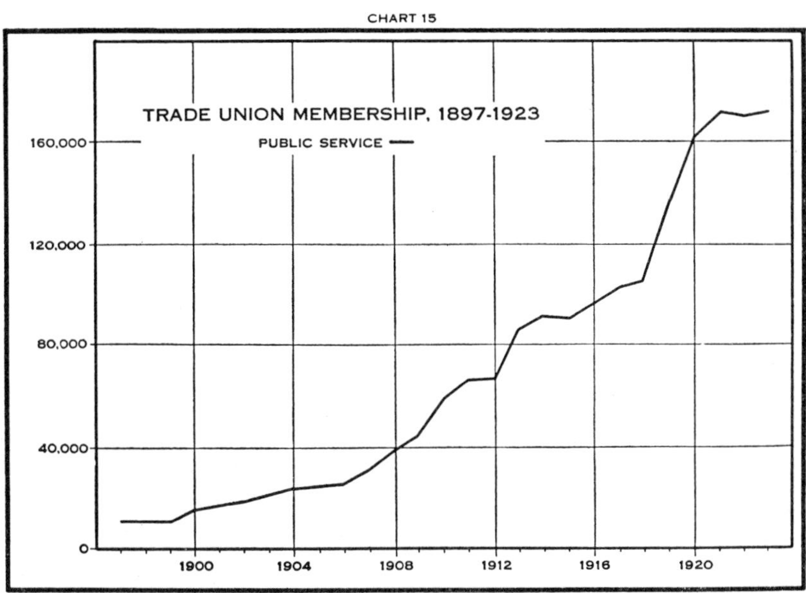

industries. By 1920, however, the transportation and metal unions had added so substantially to their absolute membership, that the building unions fell relatively in the scale to their position in 1900, although they gained more than 340,000 members from 1914 to 1920. Their position was again restored in 1923, due to the heavy losses of the metal unions and to their retention of much of their war gain. The mining group likewise lost position, not so much by reason of a drop in its own membership as because of the great absolute rise in the number of members enrolled in the other four leading groups, transportation, building, metals, clothing. The relationship among these groups in the last three years shown in the following table is further illuminated by the second table which gives for each group its actual membership. In the final year

TABLE 7.—PER CENT OF TOTAL MEMBERSHIP IN EACH GROUP OF UNIONS IN THE YEARS 1897, 1900, 1910, 1914, 1920, AND 1923

Group	1897	1900	1910	1914	1920	1923
All Groups	100.0	100.0	100.0	100.0	100.0	100.0
Transportation	26.1	21.8	22.0	20.7	24.6	25.1
Building	15.0	17.6	21.0	20.0	17.4	22.3
Metal, Machinery and Shipbuilding	11.2	9.3	9.0	8.3	16.8	9.5
Food, Liquor and Tobacco	9.9	7.6	5.3	5.0	2.3	2.3
Paper, Printing and Bookbinding	8.5	5.5	4.1	4.1	3.2	4.0
Chemical, Clay, Glass and Stone	5.2	3.5	2.8	2.1	1.0	1.2
Mining and Quarrying	4.7	15.0	12.6	14.0	8.2	11.0
Leather	3.4	1.1	2.1	2.1	2.2	1.9
Clothing	3.3	2.9	4.4	5.8	7.1	8.2
Public Service	2.5	1.8	2.7	3.4	3.2	4.5
Textile	1.8	0.9	0.9	1.1	2.9	1.0
Theatres	1.5	1.1	2.8	3.4	1.9	2.8
Restaurants and Trade	1.4	3.2	2.7	3.5	2.8	1.6
Lumber and Woodworking	1.2	2.9	1.3	0.9	0.5	0.3
Miscellaneous	4.3	5.8	6.3	5.6	5.9	4.3

building has again risen to its position of 1910 and 1914, mining once more occupies third place, and the clothing group has now forged ahead so that it is only a bit below the metal unions in rank. The food and glass and stone groups show a considerably

Group	1914	1920	1923
Transportation	561,700	1,256,100	948,300
Mining	380,200	417,700	415,400
Building	542,000	887,900	844,400
Metals	225,900	858,800	358,300
Clothing	157,000	362,400	308,400

lower rank because of both absolute and relative drops in membership.

Little need be said regarding the relative growth of the unions affiliated with the American Federation of Labor and of those independent of that organization. The essential facts appear in the chart below. Until 1900 the affiliated unions were just getting under way, whereas the independent organizations, dominated largely by the independent railroad unions, were already fairly well established. But after 1900 the spurt of the affiliated unions,

CHART 16

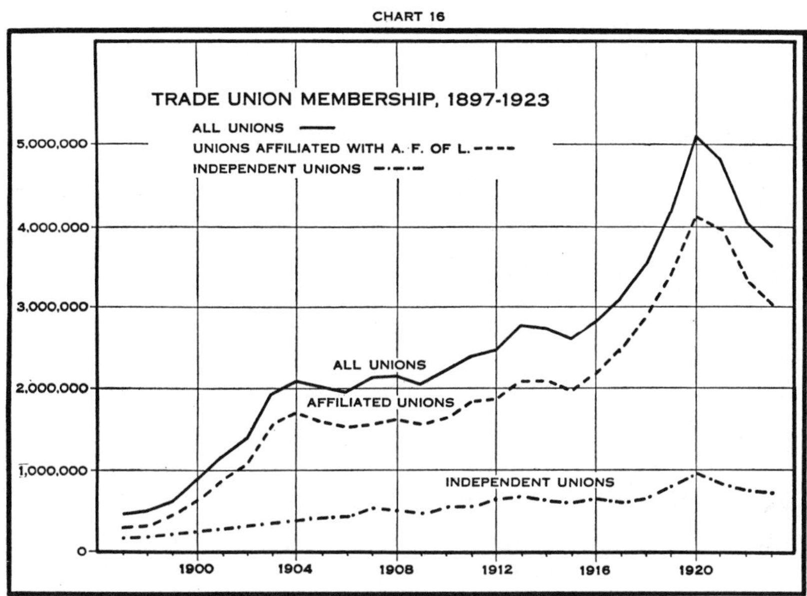

particularly the United Mine Workers, proceeded at an accelerated rate. Thus from 1897 to 1900, the mining and quarrying group moved from seventh to third place in the ranking of the groups, for its membership rose from 4.7 per cent to 15.0 per cent of the total union membership. At the same time, the transportation group fell slightly from 26.1 to 21.8 per cent of the total. During this whole movement the affiliated unions naturally gained more rapidly than the independent ones. In fact, in 1897, independents accounted for roughly 40 per cent of the total union membership, while in 1901 they constituted only 24 per cent.[1] This latter proportion has obtained practically throughout this whole period, 1901–1923, except on those occasions when the less strong affiliated unions, as from 1915–1920, made startling gains in

[1] See Table II.

membership. At those times, independent union membership represented something like one-fifth of the total. In 1923 independent membership is 19 per cent of the total. But for the effects of a major movement for independence of the American Federation of Labor, which is by no means likely, it is to be expected that the independent unions will grow more slowly than the affiliated. For the course of independent membership is almost wholly determined by the growth of the railroad brotherhoods which are by far the largest element in the independent group and which are now and have for some time in the past been near the peak of their potential maximum strength. The only perceptible and unexpected rise in the curve of independent membership in late years appeared after 1917 and was due to the inclusion of a new independent organization, the Amalgamated Clothing Workers.

An adequate interpretation of the meaning of the growth of the American labor movement in its last phase, when the changes upward and downward were of such a great magnitude, would not be complete without noting that changes of this character were apparently not limited to the United States. The period from 1914 to the present was indeed one of striking fluctuation in the membership of labor organizations throughout the world. Doubtless numerical measurement of these fluctuations will not yield accurate results, because the statistics vary considerably in reliability and because the statistical agencies of each country employ different criteria of accuracy and inclusiveness. In spite of the lack of any standards of statistical comparability, there is no avoiding the conclusion that labor organizations everywhere have experienced since the beginning of the World War an unprecedented increase in their membership.[1] The English unions, which were already very large in 1914, more than doubled their membership and by 1920 had 8,328,000 members. In Germany, France, Italy and even in South America,[2] the gains would appear to be equally striking.

As in the case of the American unions, foreign labor organiza-

[1] See Table III.

[2] Membership in Argentine, for example, is reported in the *International Labor Review* (July–Sept., 1921, p. 81) as follows: 1915, 21,000; 1916, 41,000; 1917, 159,000; 1918, 429,000; 1919, 476,000; 1920, 750,000.

TABLE 8. — MEMBERSHIP OF TRADE UNIONS IN SELECTED COUNTRIES, 1914–1923

Country	1914	1915	1916	1917	1918	1919	1920	1921	1922	1923
Australia[a]	523,271	528,031	546,556	564,187	581,755	627,685	684,450	703,009	702,938	....
Canada[b]	134,348	113,122	129,123	164,896	201,432	260,247	267,247	222,896	206,150	203,843
France[c]	1,026,000	....	....	....	....	....	1,580,967	....	1,768,461	....
Germany[d]	2,166.820	1,518,744	1,496,058	1,930,810	3,801,222	8,527,187	9,192,892	....	12,530,238	13,308,721
Italy[e]	962,000	806,000	701,000	740,000	....	1,800,000	3,100,000	....	....	....
Holland[f]	266,000	273,400	298,900	352,300	420,500	514,600	683,500	651,200	640,000	572,000
United Kingdom[g]	4,143,000	4,356,000	4,640,000	5,496,000	6,530,000	7,920,000	8,328,000	6,612,846	5,579,739	5,405,000
United States[h]	2,716,900	2,607,700	2,808,000	3,104,600	3,508,400	4,169,100	5,110,800	4,815,000	4,059,400	3,780,000

[a] *Official Year Book*, 1918, p. 989; 1923, p. 537.

[b] Department of Labour. *Labour Organization in Canada*, each year.

[c] France, Ministere du Travail, *Annuaire Statistique*, 1922, p. 217, gives the membership for *syndicats ouvrier* figures for 1914; *Bulletin*, Vol. XXX, Av-Je, 1923, p. 153, gives figures for 1920 and 1922.

[d] Germany, Statistisches Amt, *Statistisches Jahrbuch fur das Deutsche Reich*, gives the average membership for 1914 in the volume for 1916, p. 131; for 1915 in 1917, p. 179; for 1916 in 1918, p. 153; for 1917 and 1918 in 1920, p. 271; 1921–22, pp. 457 ff., figures for 1919 and 1920 are the totals of the free and Christain unions and the Hirsch-Duncker. The *Reichsarbeitsblatt*, Nichamtl. Teil, January, 1924, pp. 20–2, gives figures for 1922 and 1923.

[e] Italy, *Bolletino del Lavoro e della Previdenza Sociale*, Vol. XXXV, Jan–Je. 1921, pp. 1–258, gives figures for 1914–1917 and 1919. The figure for 1920 is taken from the *International Labour Review*, Vol. VIII, No. 1–2, p. 79.

[f] Figures obtained from Dr. Levenbach, representative in the United States of the Dutch Ministry of Labor.

[g] Great Britain, *Labour Gazette*, 1923, Vol. 31, pp. 358, 383; and 1924, Vol. 32, pp. 352, 379, gives membership figures for the end of the year. These figures exclude the Irish Free State.

[h] From Table I.

tions were also severely hit by the industrial depressions which at one time or another after the war spread nearly throughout the world. The statistics of membership for a few selected countries, drawn from original sources and presented in the preceding table, show how recessions in business and employment were accompanied by large losses in membership. English unions lost almost 3,000,000 members from 1920 to 1922. In all cases membership remained in 1922 and 1923 far above the pre-war level; and only in Australia and Germany does membership appear to have been little affected by the post-war liquidation of industry. The case of Germany is, of course, peculiar, since the labor movement after the war is placed in a setting radically different from that which prevailed in Germany before 1918.

The relation between these like movements in diverse countries is, to be sure, largely a speculative one and can be estimated finally only by an analysis of the social, economic, and political forces that appear to bear on this condition. It is important, however, in studying the situation in this country, not to overlook and, consequently, disregard the possibility of contagion in the spread of trade unionism.

CHAPTER III

THE WORKING POPULATION IN THE UNITED STATES, 1910 AND 1920

Some of the discussion in the last chapter has already indicated that statistics of the growth and decline of trade union membership may in themselves be misleading unless compared with the changes, in similar periods, of the numbers attached to industry. And a few such comparisons were made between the membership of selected unions and the changes in the number of wage earners from 1919 to 1921. Standards for evaluating, from time to time, the changing numbers or strength of a labor movement may, of course, be many; and the problem is that of choosing one which is for the present purposes most useful. The relative position of trade unionism may, for instance, be measured by comparing membership with total population, or with the number of voters in the country; or, as will be done here, with the numbers who are gainfully employed in industry.

All of these comparisons would be, unquestionably, interesting and important; but for several reasons the last appears to be the most valuable. It is possible, first, from an analysis of the last type to discover in considerable detail the sources of growth and of decline of the labor movement and thus to understand fluctuations up and down, that would be otherwise meaningless, or, at any rate, mysterious. The allocation of unions to the various industries and services, in which the people of a country work, and the study of trends of membership and of working population discloses problems and explanations, not otherwise available. This demarcation of the field, furthermore, works largely within the boundaries which the trade unions have laid out for themselves. Their strength, and numbers, and control are the subject of inquiry in the areas where they have staked out their claims; and although their claims are often vague and ill-defined, the problems so raised are not difficult to settle and indeed elicit new and even more significant problems. The working population in a country may, finally, pursue a course quite distinct from that of the total population. It may either increase or decline more rapidly than the total population; or large sections of it, more or less accessible to labor organization, may come to occupy a leading or subordinate position in the work of the country. Phenomena, such as these, which would be otherwise concealed are brought to light by drawing the comparison between the numbers of workers and the numbers of trade union members.

Sources of information concerning the working population of the United States are likewise many. From the federal censuses of manufactures, before 1919 quinquennial and since biennial, can be obtained the numbers who work in the manufacturing industries; the Interstate Commerce Commission publishes annual reports containing detailed information on the laboring forces of the steam railroad system; and the annual reports of the United States Geological Survey present the statistics of the number at work in mines. While each of these agencies produces statistical material of a very high order of excellence, they are in two respects inferior for the purposes of this study to the statistics furnished by the federal census of occupations. This document, based on the decennial census of population, is in the first place exhaustive. It includes statistics for all industry, agriculture, transportation, trade, and all forms of service, that bring pecuniary income. It thus makes available data for such groups as the building trades and commercial occupations, which are not included in any of the above sources, and for the whole field of service, like professional and domestic service, for which there is no other source of information. Secondly, defective as a decennial census of occupations may be in accuracy, its elements are comparable for each census period since, in the main, the same standards of enumeration and classification are applied to all of its constituent elements. Statistics drawn from separate and independent sources would lose in comparability what they might gain in reliability. For these reasons the major comparisons in the following pages are made between the membership of trade unions and the number of occupied persons reported in the decennial censuses of occupations.

The census of occupations, nevertheless, also has its defects.[1] It has first the defect common to any census, that its data are applicable to only a short period of time. The census of occupations of 1920, for example, reveals the state of affairs only during the first two weeks in January of that year. Conditions then may not have been representative of the whole year; or they may have been quite representative for some classifications, within the census, and less representative for others. This is often, as will be seen later, precisely what happens. Furthermore, the whole decennial census, as well as the occupation census, is still in the hands of a large number of untrained enumerators. Occupation enumeration is a task requiring at least a minimum of technical skill and knowledge. The overlapping of occupations, the prevalence of a vague and frequently inconsistent terminology, require of enumerators insight and discrimination which can come only from training and experience. Lacking such enumerators, the results are likely to be, and in fact are, subject to considerable error.

There are, indeed, persisting types of error, due to unskilled enumeration, which are recognized by the Census and which are discussed periodically in the decennial reports on occupation statistics. For instance, factory operatives frequently report their old trade names, such as bakers, tailors, and there consequently results an overestimate of the number of bakers, millers, jewelers, tailors and tailoresses. Clerks in stores are often not distinguished from salesmen and saleswomen. Locomotive engineers and fire-

[1] Dr. Wolman having accounted for the membership in American trade unions, naturally desired to compare their memberships with the total number of workers according to occupations. In order to do so the only possible source was the reports of the Census. It is well recognized that the Census reports on this subject are unreliable. There is in the first place confusion between principles of industrial classification and occupational. In the second place enumerations are made carelessly. And in the third place the statistician has to deal with shifting conditions, in that workers change from one industry to another and from one occupation to another. Dr. Wolman has regrouped the Census statistics in order to eliminate certain manifest incongruities, but obviously such work can be nothing more than the exercise of judgment. Another statistician might obtain different results. Such work resolves itself into an expression of probability, and in no sense to a determination of fact. The basic data are of such nature that from them no facts can be determined.

It is important that these conditions should be understood lest the National Bureau of Economic Research be considered as endorsing as facts what it knows to be doubtful. It may be that Dr. Wolman's correlation of membership in trade unions with probable occupational numbers is near enough for practical purposes. We may reasonably assume that it is. His findings in such terms, however, are to be viewed as those of an intelligent reconnaissance rather than as something of definite scientific determination.—Note by Walter Renton Ingalls.

men are frequently confused with stationary firemen and engineers. In the group of domestic and personal service, careful distinction is not made between cooks and general servants; housewives not receiving wages and working at home are returned as housekeepers and stewardesses; the classification of the various kinds of nurses is not successful. Within a major division of industry, it is found difficult to distinguish clearly the constituent groups. From the returns in the clothing industry it is hard to differentiate the employees in the various branches of that industry. Similar problems are encountered in the other industries as well.[1]

Any occupation census, moreover, is useful to the degree in which it is comparable to an earlier or a later census. As instructions to enumerators are changed for the purpose of improving the returns and as the system of classification is modified, comparison becomes difficult and more uncertain. This is the case with regard to any two successive censuses; and it is true also with regard to the censuses of 1910 and 1920, which will be used in this and later chapters. The signal difference between the censuses of occupations of 1920 and 1910 lies in the change in the date of enumeration. The census of 1920 shows conditions in early January and that of 1910 in the middle of April. The change admittedly confuses comparison by the introduction of a seasonal element, for such items, particularly, as agriculture and building, known to exist but exceedingly hard to measure. Obviously the injection of an indeterminate variant like this makes somewhat difficult the task of measuring growth and decline.

The 1910 census, moreover, afforded a much more detailed classification of occupations than is offered by the 1920 census. In the earlier census, occupations were classified within each industrial division into employer and supervisory group, clerical occupations, occupations not peculiar to the industry and occupations peculiar to the industry. For the cotton manufacturing industry, for example, it was possible in the 1910 census to derive directly from the printed tables the number of employers and supervisors, the number of clerical and office workers associated with cotton manufacturing establishments, the number of persons, like machinists, not peculiar to that industry who worked in and around cotton

[1] Fourteenth Census of the United States, 1920, Vol. IV, *Occupations*, p. 14 ff.

factories, and finally the number of strictly cotton manufactory operatives. With this highly detailed material it was, of course, possible to make most illuminating groupings and rearrangements. This elaborate classification is in large part discarded in the 1920 census, because the returns on which it was based are not regarded as sufficiently trustworthy. In its place the last census of occupations presents pretty much the same list of industries and sub-industries, and reports for each the numbers of semi-skilled persons and laborers there employed. Gross figures, which do not indicate the industries to which the members of the occupation are attached, are reported for such general occupations as carpenters, machinists, bricklayers, molders, painters; and there are reported the numbers in such categories as "manufacturers," distributed among the major divisions of industry like "extraction of minerals" and "manufacturing industries," but not apportioned to the sub-industries, like "iron and steel," "textiles," or "food."

Without stopping at this time to analyze the census figures any further, it would be well to give the outstanding results in 1910 and 1920, as reported by the Bureau of the Census. For the first time since 1880, the 1920 census shows a relative fall in the rate of increase of the gainfully occupied population of the United States in the decade from 1910 to 1920. The table [1] below shows that

Year	Persons 10 Years of Age and Over Engaged in Gainful Occupations		
	Number	Per Cent of Total Population	Per Cent of Population 10 Years of Age and Over
1920	41,614,248	39.4	50.3
1910	38,167,336	41.5	53.3
1900	29,073,233	38.3	50.2
1890	23,318,183	37.2	49.2
1880	17,392,099	34.7	47.3

while there was an increase in the absolute numbers of persons 10 years of age and over gainfully engaged in industry from 1910

[1] 1920 Census of Occupations, p. 33.

to 1920, the rate of increase in the number of occupied persons relative to that of the population slackened. This retardation in the rate of increase the Census regards as real, since it is general throughout the country, except in Michigan and the District of Columbia, and ascribes to a number of causes. The most important cause it considers the change in the census date from 1910 to 1920, which found some important occupational divisions in the latter year at their low ebb of employment. In these cases the enumerators apparently reported many persons who were unemployed but probably still attached to the industry as unoccupied. Another factor was the more rigid enforcement of child labor laws and the spread of this type of restrictive legislation, which reduced appreciably the numbers reported in the age group 10–15. The most striking changes took place in agriculture where there were actually fewer persons engaged in 1920 than in 1910; the Census reporting a drop of roughly 1,700,000 persons. A large but unestimated portion of this decrease, the Census ascribes to overenumeration of certain groups in 1910 and to underenumeration of certain groups in 1920. It believes, also, that the war led to a substantial shifting of labor from farm to factory and that this redistribution of the working population is revealed in the drop in 1920 of the number engaged in agricultural pursuits.[1]

For a considerable period of time, agriculture, in terms of the relative numbers of persons gainfully engaged, has increased much less rapidly than the industrial and commercial groups. The large absolute and relative drop in agriculture in the last intercensal period has, of course, accentuated this movement and agriculture stands lower in the entire industrial picture in 1920 than ever before. The next table,[2] which shows the relative rank of the general divisions of occupations in 1910 and 1920, reveals the changing status of agriculture and other important groups during that decade. The striking changes of the period are the drop in agriculture, both the absolute and relative drop in the group of domestic and personal service, and the very large rise, absolutely and relatively, in manufacturing and mechanical industries, and in clerical occupations.

[1] For a full discussion of these points, see 1920 Occupation Census, pp. 18–24.
[2] *Ibid.*, p. 34.

TABLE 9.—INDUSTRIAL DISTRIBUTION OF PERSONS ENGAGED IN GAINFUL OCCUPATIONS
1920 AND 1910

General Division of Occupations	Total Persons 10 Years of Age and Over Engaged in Gainful Occupations			
	1920		1910	
	Number	Per Cent Distribution	Number	Per Cent Distribution
All Occupations	41,614,248	100.0	38,167,336	100.0
Agriculture, Forestry, Animal Husbandry	10,953,158	26.3	12,659,082	33.2
Extraction of Minerals	1,090,223	2.6	965,169	2.5
Manufacturing and Mechanical	12,818,524	30.8	10,628,731	27.8
Transportation	3,063,582	7.4	2,637,420	6.9
Trade	4,242,979	10.2	3,614,670	9.5
Public Service (not elsewhere classified)	770,460	1.9	459,291	1.2
Professional Service	2,143,889	5.2	1,693,361	4.4
Domestic and Personal Service	3,404,892	8.2	3,772,559	9.9
Clerical Occupations	3,126,541	7.5	1,737,053	4.6

In order to examine in greater detail the nature of the rates of rise and decline since 1910, the figures for both census years, as they appear in the 1920 census, were recast into a slightly larger number of groups and the per cent of change in the number in each group from 1910 to 1920 was computed. The results are presented in the next table; and they show that, while the total population, 10 years of age and over, increased 15.6 per cent, the total number gainfully engaged in industry increased just slightly more than 9 per cent. It is the distribution of this increase among the constituent groups, however, that is interesting and significant. Thus manufacturing industries, which next to agriculture is the most numerous category, rose from 1910 to 1920 at a rate considerably faster than that of the population 10 years of age and over. Clerical occupations, likewise, including more than 1,500,000 persons in 1910 and nearly 3,000,000 in 1920, grew much more rapidly than population. Trade and professional service, which between them include from 5,000,000 to 6,000,000 persons, exceeded appreciably the rate of population increase; while the rate of growth of transportation and mining was only slightly slower than that of the population. The marked decline, both relatively and absolutely, came in the building trades, domestic and personal service, and in agricultural pursuits. But it is in precisely these occupations that the 1920 census is least comparable to the census of 1910.

TABLE 10. — CHANGES IN NUMBER ENGAGED IN GAINFUL OCCUPATIONS
1910 TO 1920

General Division of Occupations	Per Cent Change 1910 to 1920
Extraction of Minerals	13.0
Manufacturing Industries	31.6
Transportation	12.9
Building Trades	– 6.1
Stationary Engineers	4.8
Stationary Firemen	29.3
Trade	21.7
Professional Service	26.6
Domestic and Personal Service	– 9.9
Clerical Occupations	80.8
Public Service (not elsewhere classified)	68.3
Agriculture, Forestry, and Animal Husbandry	– 13.5
Total	9.3

The building industry is subject to violent seasonal fluctuations, and the 1920 census was taken in early January, whereas the preceding census was taken in the middle of April, a comparatively open season for construction. The results for agriculture were influenced not alone by possible seasonal factors, but also by thoroughgoing modifications in the methods of enumeration. The occupations that fall in the category of domestic and personal service are notoriously difficult to enumerate and are, therefore, probably subject to a substantial margin of error. In the light of these observations, conclusions concerning the trends in the size of the working population of the United States between the years 1910 and 1920 require further scrutiny and analysis. Except, however, for probable inaccuracies in reporting certain categories in agriculture, the census statistics of occupations, in general, appear to be reliable enough for the purposes of this inquiry.

Since the trade union movement is composed of organizations of persons who work for wages and whose industrial status is tolerably clear, any fair estimate of the strength of the movement would be derived from a comparison between its membership and the number of employed persons in the country who have, as nearly as can be determined from the statistics of occupations, the status of wage earners. In order to obtain figures for the total number of wage earners in all industry, service, and agriculture in 1910 and 1920, the occupation statistics for those years, presented in the 1920 census, were recast into the following classifications: employers and self-employed, salaried persons, and wage earners. This regrouping was naturally not accomplished without difficulty and without frequent arbitrary decision. Where the census reports such a group as "employers," the case is, of course, clear. With regard to such an item as "officials," however, it is sometimes doubtful whether those included in the group fall within the salaried or employer group, or in both. Since no data for making the distribution were available, it was assumed that all members of the "official" group were in the supervisory or salaried class. In general the salaried class was restricted to those occupations that appeared to be supervisory or managerial and to those members of the professional group who worked for employers.

The employer and self-employed class was limited to owners, persons working for themselves and persons like doctors and lawyers, in the professional service groups, who may be regarded as the fee-receiving class. The greatest difficulty in determining the constitution of this group was found in allocating to it portions of such occupations as dressmakers, milliners, shoemakers, tailors, where it was impossible to determine from the available data how many were self-employed and how many worked for employers. In all of these cases, arbitrary decisions were made after a careful study of the classified indexes of occupations of the 1920 census.[1]

[1]*Classified Index to Occupations*, Fourteenth Census, 1920, and *Alphabetical Index to Occupations*, Fourteenth Census, 1920.

The wage earner group is composed of all occupied persons described in the census as "semi-skilled" and "laborers"; of persons working at such industrial occupations as bricklayers, carpenters, locomotive engineers; of clerks, bookkeepers, salesmen and saleswomen in stores, stenographers and typists; and of farm laborers.

The general results of this reclassification of the census figures are taken from Table IV of the Appendix to this book and are presented in the next tabulation. From this tabulation it would appear that the total number of wage earners constituted 62.7 per cent of the total number of gainfully engaged persons in 1920 and 58.7 per cent in 1910; the salaried group represented 8.5 per cent in 1920 and 6.5 per cent in 1910; and the employer and self-employed group 28.8 per cent in 1920 and 34.7 per cent in 1910. Judging largely from the character of the raw data and the way in which these groups were made up, it is highly probable that, in both 1920 and 1910, the numbers in the employer and self-employed group were exaggerated at the expense of the numbers in the salaried group. Some who seem to be described in the census as employers or self-employed persons are unquestionably salaried persons engaged in supervisory and managerial functions. While there are also a number designated as officials and now placed in the salaried group, who properly belong among the employers and self-employed, their number is relatively small in comparison with the former. A fairer comparison, then, is between the total number of wage earners and the aggregate number in both the employers and self-employed, and salaried groups. If this comparison is made, it is found that of the total working population in 1920, 62.7 per cent were wage earners and 37.3 per cent non wage earners; whereas in 1910, 58.7 were wage earners and 41.3 per cent salaried persons and employers. These conclusions, also, need to be accepted with caution. There is good internal evidence that a number of persons, probably between 5 and 10 per cent, included in the group of wage earners, in both census years properly belong in either the employer or salaried classes. There is, however, no exact method for estimating the number of such persons for either census year or for measuring the disparities in this regard as between the two censuses.

TABLE 11.—DISTRIBUTION OF WORKING POPULATION INTO EMPLOYER, SALARIED AND WAGE-EARNING CLASSES
1920 AND 1910

	1920	1910
Employers and Self-Employed	11,974,369	13,175,711
Extraction of Minerals	17,334	14,287
Manufacturing Industries	562,199	814,974
Transportation	81,488	59,572
Building Trades	90,109	174,422
Trade	1,786,902	1,530,340
Professional Service	758,336	612,444
Domestic and Personal Service	426,688	512,081
Agriculture, etc	8,251,313	9,457,591
Salaried (supervisory and professional)	3,540,608	2,482,478
Extraction of Minerals	53,922	34,285
Manufacturing Industries	557,363	300,792
Transportation	212,228	160,091
Trade	524,014	396,721
Professional Service	1,237,286	999,251
Domestic and Personal Service	52,736	57,273
Public Service (not elsewhere classified)	801,826	476,347
Agriculture, etc	101,233	14,345
Wage Earners (manual and clerical workers)	26,080,689	22,406,714
Extraction of Minerals	1,018,967	916,597
Manufacturing Industries	8,775,543	6,401,436
Transportation	2,962,614	2,664,674
Building Trades	2,397,391	2,475,329
Stationary Engineers	242,096	231,041
Stationary Firemen	143,875	111,248
Trade	1,937,600	1,563,117
Professional Service	148,267	81,666
Domestic and Personal Service	2,902,955	3,185,907
Clerical Workers	2,950,769	1,631,926
Agriculture	2,600,612	3,143,773

The figures just cited for the numbers included in the employer and self-employed group may seem to be disproportionately large. The largest single item in this group, however, is the agriculture, forestry and animal husbandry class, which contained 8,251,313 persons in 1920 and 9,457,591 in 1910. If these figures are deducted from the total for the group, the category of employers and self-employed stands at 3,723,056 in 1920 and at 3,680,120 in 1910. Thus the effect of omitting agriculture is to leave the group larger in 1920 than in 1910. In the construction of these groups, two decisions were made concerning which there might conceivably be wide difference of opinion. Farm laborers, working on home farms, were in both census years included in the agricultural employer group. This added in 1920 to that group, 1,850,119 persons and in 1910, 3,310,534 persons. Secondly, the professional group was split into three parts. Those items designated by the census as "semi-professional pursuits" and "attendants and helpers (professional service)" were placed in the category of wage earners. Those left in the census group of "professional service" were distributed, after a careful examination of the specific occupations, roughly, in the proportion of 38 and 62 per cent respectively to the employer and self-employed, and salaried groups.

The results obtained by this recasting of the statistics of occupations of the United States Census do not in all particulars agree with the conclusions reached in another study of the same subject conducted in the National Bureau of Economic Research. Dr. W. I. King, in connection with his studies of the national income, has, for a longer series of years, classified the working population of the United States into much the same categories as are here presented. A comparison of Dr. King's figures and those of this study is shown in the following table. The existing differences between these sets of figures arise from two sources. Except for his estimate of the number included in the employer and self-employed group, Dr. King's statistics represent averages for the year, whereas the other set is referable to the census period January 1 to January 15, 1920. Dr. King's figures, moreover, are drawn from many places. His data are estimates based not alone on the statistics of the census of occupations, but also on the statistics of occupations of the censuses of manufactures, of the reports of the Interstate Commerce Commission and the Geological Survey, and on other statistical reports. The figures in the last column, however, are estimates drawn almost solely from the returns of the census of occupations, because it was deemed desirable to use as the

TABLE 12. — COMPARISON OF CLASSIFICATIONS OF THE WORKING POPULATION OF THE UNITED STATES
1920

Group	King	Wolman[d]
Employers and Self-Employed	10,029,274[a]	10,124,250
Home Farm Laborers	[b]	1,850,119
Wage Earners (manual and clerical workers)	....	26,080,689
Wage Earners (excluding clerical workers)	23,058,191[c]	....
Salaried (supervisory and professional)	....	3,540,608
Salaried (including clerical workers)	6,900,809[c]	....
Total	39,988,274	41,595,666

[a] As of December 31, 1919.
[b] This group King omits from his figures.
[c] Average for year 1920.
[d] Figures in this column, taken from the Census of Occupations, 1920, are as of January 1–15, 1920.

basis for comparison with trade union membership the results of a census count.

Another elaborate reclassification of the census of occupations for 1920 was made by Carl Hookstadt in 1923.[1] In this study, he recasts the occupation statistics into groups of employees, officials and managers, and employers and independent workers, within the framework of the industrial classification employed by the census. He reclassified, also, the statistics of occupations in accordance with the main industrial classifications adopted by the International Association of Industrial Accident Boards and Commissions. A comparison of Hookstadt's gross totals with those derived from Tabel IV in the Appendix of this study is given in the accompanying table. The outstanding differences appear in the number of employees, which is, roughly, 3,000,000, larger in the Hookstadt tabulation; and in the number of salaried persons which is 2,600,000 greater in the present author's classification. The principal sources of these discrepancies are two. Mr. Hookstadt breaks up the group of professional service and throws the bulk of it into his employee class. But in the grouping here adopted, more than 1,200,000 persons of the professional service group are placed in the salaried class. The difference is one merely of definition. The

[1] *Monthly Labor Review*, U. S. Department of Labor, July, 1923, p. 1.

TABLE 13. — COMPARISON OF TWO CLASSIFICATIONS OF UNITED STATES CENSUS OF OCCUPATIONS, 1920

Industry	Hookstadt			Wolman		
	Employees	Officials and Managers	Employers, Independent Workers, etc.	Wage Earners (Manual and clerical workers)	Salaried (Supervisory and professional)	Employers and Self-Employed
Agriculture, Forestry, Animal Husbandry	2,699,064	2,095	8,251,999	2,600,612	101,233	8,251,313
Extraction of Minerals	1,055,898	16,991	17,334	1,018,967	53,922	17,334
Manufacturing and Mechanical Industries	11,869,506	249,950	699,068	8,775,543	557,363	562,199
Building Trades	....	......	....	2,393,391	....	90,109
Transportation	2,857,796	73,172	132,614	2,962,614	212,228	81,488
Trade	2,439,673	342,120	1,461,186	1,937,600	524,014	1,786,902
Public Service (not elsewhere classified)	614,270	156,190	....	....	801,826	....
Professional Service	1,434,487	11,655	697,747	148,267	1,237,286	758,336
Domestic and Personal Service	2,871,115	56,021	477,756	2,902,955	52,736	426,688
Clerical Occupations	3,126,541	......	....	2,950,769	....	....
Stationary Engineers	....	......	....	242,096	....	....
Stationary Firemen	....	......	....	143,875	....	....
Total	28,968,350	908,194	11,737,704	26,080,689	3,540,608	11,974,369

second large source of difference arises from diverse methods of treating such groups as foremen and supervisors. In the group of "extraction of minerals," for example, the foremen, overseers, and inspectors are placed by Mr. Hookstadt in his employee class, and in this study in the salaried class. This difference in approach obtains throughout the various classifications of industry and accounts largely for the excess in the number of employees in the Hookstadt tabulation. Granting the assumptions made here in distributing the persons gainfully engaged in industry among these three classes, and assuming further that there still remains a substantial number in the wage-earner class who are engaged in managerial and supervisory functions or who are self-employed, it would appear that the total number of wage earners in the United States in early January, 1920, should be put in round numbers at 25,000,000.

CHAPTER IV

THE EXTENT OF LABOR ORGANIZATION IN 1910 AND 1920

Even the number of wage earners, as defined in the last chapter, would not be considered by some a thoroughly fair base for measuring the achievement in size of an organized labor movement. The final figure there derived includes agricultural employees, whom trade unions have made little effort to organize, and such other groups, like clerical workers, whose adherence to the trade union is of comparatively recent origin. Trade unions, moreover, limit their membership in a great variety of ways. Almost all exclude persons not yet of a specified age; some have standards of skill which prospective members must meet; others impose high initiation fees or require attachment to the industry for a specified period of years; and still others impose restrictions on entry based on the color and sex of the applicants to membership. The extent of trade unionism would naturally appear in its most favorable statistical light, if allowance were made for these various factors and trade union membership were compared only with the residuum of organizable employees. No attempt is, however, here made to deal with such refinements; and comparison is always made between the numbers in trade unions and the numbers of those employees, who are, by common consent, regarded as likely material for organization in trade unions.

Computing the percentage that union membership represents of the total number of wage earners in the United States and of the number in the major and minor divisions of industry involves technical difficulties, which cannot be altogether overcome. The most serious of these is encountered in the attempt to make the statistics of membership conform to the statistics of occupations. Union membership, since many unions are organized along trade or occupational lines, frequently overlaps the industrial classes of the census.

Although nearly all labor organizations have most elaborate official statements of their jurisdictional claims, it is generally impossible, except by arbitrary decision, to split their membership among the various industrial classifications of the census. The carpenters' union, for instance, as has already been pointed out, includes in its membership not only building carpenters but also factory workers employed in the industry, described by the census as "lumber and its manufactures." While it is possible to effect a distribution, in round numbers, of the total membership of this union into the number working on buildings and those in factories, finer estimates are impracticable. The same holds true of other important unions. The difficulty encountered in separating the self-employed from those employed by others, which is a real one in many industries and occupations, has already been discussed.

The detailed materials for computing the percentage organized among the various divisions of industry and among selected occupations and the results of those computations are presented in the Appendix to this volume in Tables V, VI, VII, VIII and IX. The first table of this series shows the membership of every American national and international union in the year 1920. It differs from the first exhaustive table of membership (Table I) in that it contains also the Canadian membership of each American organization which has jurisdiction over workers in Canadian industry. From it are derived the statistics of the membership in the United States alone of the unions included in the table. Since the occupation census gives statistics only for the continental United States, comparison can properly be made only with the United States membership of labor organizations.

Actual comparisons between membership and the number of wage earners in the year 1920 are shown in Table VI. This table was constructed by separating for each industry and subdivision of industry in the census of occupations of 1920 the wage earners from the salaried and employer classes. Next to these figures were placed the statistics of trade union membership in the United States taken from Table V. It will be found that the number of wage earners in certain industries differs substantially from the statistics of Table IV. This is due largely to the fact that the jurisdiction claims of the unions forced the inclusion in Table VI of several categories of workers who were clearly employed in managerial or supervisory functions and who were, consequently, properly classified in Table IV in the salaried group. The final percentages of organization underestimate somewhat the prevailing extent of organization in 1920 because of the omission of independent local unions, whose membership could not be obtained, and of local unions directly affiliated with the American Federation of Labor, whose membership could not, through the lack of the necessary data, be distributed among the industries of the country. The net effects of these omissions are almost imperceptible and are not likely to change the present results by any more than one per cent.[1]

Similar statistics showing the percentage of organization in 1910 are given in Table VII. This table is reprinted, substantially in its original form, from the article already cited.[2] It has, however, been revised in several important particulars to meet differences between the census of 1910 and that of 1920. It has been pointed out before that the occupation statistics of 1910 were in much more detailed form than those of 1920. It was possible in the earlier census to make finer classifications than could be used in dealing with the later census. For this reason consolidated classifications replaced the more detailed ones in the original table. In some instances apparent improvements in classification dictated modifications in the original 1910 table. Thus coopers were taken from the "hand trades," which are altogether omitted from the revised table, and were put into the lumber and furniture industries. The large category of electric light and power plants, electric supply factories, electricians and electrical engineers, telegraph and tele-

[1] The membership of the I. W. W. was, also, omitted from the table because it was made available too late. The office of the I. W. W. reports its membership to have been distributed in 1920 as follows:

Lumber Workers	7,000
Agricultural Workers	6,000
Mine Workers	4,600
General Construction Workers	5,500
Railroad Workers	4,700
House and Building Construction Workers	3,800
Metal and Machinery Workers	4,000
Marine Transport Workers	6,000
Total	41,600

[2] *Quarterly Journal of Economics*, May, 1916, p. 606.

phone linemen, was split into a number of diverse elements and the membership of the electrical workers' union, originally allotted to this comprehensive group, was reapportioned to the new industrial classes. The most radical revisions in the original table were made for the general occupational divisions of "trade," "public service," "professional service," "domestic and personal service," "agriculture, forestry and animal husbandry," "proprietary, supervisory and official" groups, and "clerical" groups. All of these groupings and classifications contained in the original table were completely discarded and were replaced by revised figures for both 1910 and 1920, taken entirely from the census of occupations of 1920. In their present form, Tables VI and VII, showing respectively percentages of labor organization in 1920 and 1910, possess a high degree of comparability.

Compared with the total numbers of wage earners in this country, trade union strength as measured by its membership was relatively twice as great in 1920 as in 1910. The rate of growth during this decade was approximately the same whether membership is compared with the industrial wage-earning population of the country or with the combined industrial and agricultural wage-earning population. The tabulation below shows that, roughly, one-

	Total Wage Earners	Trade Union Membership in U. S.	Per Cent Organized	Total Wage Earners Excluding Agriculture	Trade Union Membership in U. S.	Per Cent Organized
1920...	26,080,689	4,881,200	18.7	23,480,077	4,881,200	20.8
1910...	22,406,714	2,101,502	9.4	19,262,941	2,101,502	10.9

fifth of the wage earners of the country were members of labor organizations; whereas in 1910 something like one-tenth were so organized. In other words in 1920, after 10 years of very substantial growth in numbers, about four-fifths of the general category of wage earners were not members of unions. While these figures are in themselves of considerable interest, their full significance cannot be clear without detailed inquiry into the sources of union strength and weakness. Such inquiry can be conducted only by discovering the varying magnitude of trade unionism in the great divisions of industry.

It has long been generally appreciated that labor organizations receive their first impetus and make their most striking headway among the so-called manual workers, those who work in factories and mines, on railroads and buildings; and that they have their most retarded development among persons, sometimes described as white-collar workers, who embrace unionism late and slowly. This appears to be universally true. An examination of the extent of labor organization among these two types of employees in 1910 and 1920 shows this to have been the case in the United States as well. While the percentage of total employees who are members of unions is, roughly, 20, all of the important manual labor groups stood far above this level; and in 1910 when the general percentage of organization was approximately 10, the same groups of

TABLE 14. — PER CENT OF WAGE EARNERS ORGANIZED IN MAJOR DIVISIONS OF INDUSTRY
1920 AND 1910

Division of Industry	Per Cent Organized	
	1920	1910
Extraction of Minerals	41.0	27.3
Manufacturing Industries	23.2	11.6
Transportation	37.3	17.1
Building Trades	25.5	16.4
Stationary Engineers	12.4	4.6
Stationary Firemen	19.9	9.6
Trade	1.1	1.0
Professional Service	5.4	4.6
Clerical Occupations	8.3	1.8
Domestic and Personal Service	3.8	2.0
Public Service	7.3	2.5

manual laborers all showed a higher percentage of organization. The total percentage of organization is in both census years considerably reduced by the absence of many large labor organizations in trade, professional service, clerical occupations, domestic and personal service, and public service. Membership in the manual workers' groups represented almost 28 and 15 per cent of the wage earners in those groups in 1920 and 1910; whereas membership among the non-factory workers was in the same years less than 5 and 2 per cent of all persons engaged in those occupations. Growth, from 1910 to 1920, occurred in all groups, but it was greatest in manufacturing, transportation, clerical occupations, and public service; although the rise in mining and in the building trades was also considerable.

Differences in the extent of organization among the industries that comprise these major divisions are quite as striking and as significant as the differences among the major divisions themselves. At the same time that the whole mining group showed an increase in the extent of organization from 27 to 41, coal mines increased their organization from 35 per cent to nearly 51, while trade unionism in copper, gold and other mines actually had a lower percentage of organization in 1920 than in 1910. The strength of the Western Federation of Miners has not been regained by its successor, the Mine, Mill and Smelter Workers' Union. In 1910 the workers in the salt, oil and natural gas industry had no union at all; in 1920 there was a substantial organization with a membership of over 20,000. Such analysis can be pushed even further. Thus the average number of coal miners in the United States in 1920 was 784,621, of which 639,547 were bituminous and 145,074 anthracite miners.[1] It is known that the anthracite miners have a much higher degree of organization than the soft coal miners. Bituminous miners were, therefore, in 1920 probably less than 50 per cent organized.

Extent of organization in manufacturing industries runs the whole gamut from less than 1 per cent of organization in the chemical and allied industries to more than 57 per cent in clothing. The tremendous rise in the percentage of organization in this industry is, in fact, the most striking phenomenon in the whole group of manufacturing industries. The clothing industry was converted from one of the weakly organized industries in 1910 into one of the most strongly organized in 1920. This is attributable, mainly, as was shown in the discussion of the growth of membership in this group, to the rise of the International Ladies' Garment Workers

[1] U. S. Geological Survey, *Mineral Resources of the United States*, Part II. "Coal in 1919, 1920, and 1921," p. 494.

TABLE 15. — PER CENT OF ORGANIZATION AMONG DIVISIONS OF MANUFACTURING INDUSTRIES
1920 AND 1910

Industry	Per Cent Organized	
	1920	1910
Manufacturing Industries	23.2	11.6
Chemical and Allied	0.2	1.4
Clay, Glass and Stone	21.5	20.5
Clothing	57.8	16.9
Food and Kindred Products	19.4	7.6
Iron and Steel	28.1	10.4
Leather	29.4	14.6
Liquor and Beverage	....	67.6
Lumber	18.1	10.3
Metal (except Iron and Steel)	12.9	6.5
Paper and Pulp	7.9	2.6
Printing and Publishing	50.1	34.3
Textile	15.0	3.7
Cigar and Tobacco	29.2	26.9

after their strike in 1910 and to the rapid increase in membership of the Amalgamated Clothing Workers, after their organization in the last months of 1914.

The group of clay, glass and stone industries, although it experienced apparently a very slight gain in this decade really suffered a substantial loss in one of its constituents. Extent of organization in the glass industry fell from 34.2 per cent in 1910 to 27.9 in 1920; at the same time marble and stone yards increased only very slightly from 45.4 to 47.7 per cent, while potteries and brick, tile and terra cotta factories made more substantial gains. The latter were, however, hardly organized in 1910 and even in 1920 had achieved organization of only 9 per cent.

The very large rise in the food group was due almost wholly to an enormous growth in the extent of organization in slaughter and packing houses, or, in other words, in the packing industry. This industry had organization in 1910 of something over 6 per cent; but in 1920 it had grown to nearly 60 per cent. Butter and cheese factories, candy factories, flour and grain mills, sugar refineries had practically no organization at all, either in 1910 or in 1920. Bakeries were less than one-fifth organized.

Figures for the iron and steel industry appear to contradict current conceptions of the status of labor organization in that industry and are somewhat misleading, although the growth from 1910 to 1920 is a real one. In that portion of the steel industry which manufactures basic iron and steel products, there was very little labor organization in either 1910 or 1920, in spite of the fact that the membership of the Amalgamated Association of Iron, Steel and Tin Workers, the most important union in this branch of the industry, was much larger in 1920 than in 1910. The category of iron and steel industries here presented, however, includes the manufacture of iron and steel products, such as agricultural implements, automobiles, railroad cars, ships and boats, as well as individual occupations such as blacksmiths, boilermakers, pattern makers, iron molders, machinists. In these branches of the industry there was substantial organization in both census years, and marked growth from one to the other; but it is unfortunate that the form of the trade union statistics does not permit the calculation of the percentage organized in each of these branches of the iron and steel industry. The figures for metal, except iron and steel, suffer from much the same defect of representing too conglomerate an industry.

The classification of the liquor and beverage industries followed by the census in 1910 and 1920 seems to be so radically different, that there appears to be no sound basis of comparison. In 1910 this was one of the most strongly organized industries in the country. While the brewery workers' union is still in existence, it is now a weak organization, known as the United Brewery, Flour, Cereal and Soft Drink Workers' Union, with little more than 15,000 members in the soft drink industry, 1,000 in the cider, vinegar, yeast and alcohol industries, 800 in the flour and cereal industries, and 150 in the syrup industry.

With few exceptions those parts of the manufacturing industries which were well organized in 1910 had strengthened their organization by 1920. The printing and publishing industry which was a little better than one-third organized in 1910 achieved organization of more than one-half in 1920. The great basic industries like chemicals, iron and steel, food products, lumber, metals, paper and pulp, and textiles were, after the total growth from 1910 to 1920, even in the most favorable instances less than one-fifth organized. The striking exceptions were, on the one hand, the clothing and packing industries, in which organization attained an entirely new and higher level, and, on the other, the liquor and beverage industries where uncommon, but well-known circumstances, prevailed, that led to disintegration of the union.

Transportation industries show in general a higher level of organization than the manufacturing industries. In fact, the three most substantial elements of this group were all more than 50 per cent organized in 1920 and had more than doubled their percentage of organization since 1910. The most striking change took place in the division of water transportation where the percentage organized rose from less than 30 to more than 85, due very largely to spectacular leaps in membership among longshoremen and seamen.

TABLE 16.—PER CENT OF ORGANIZATION AMONG DIVISIONS OF THE TRANSPORTATION INDUSTRY
1920 AND 1910

Industry	Per Cent Organized	
	1920	1910
All Transportation	37.3	17.1
Water Transportation	85.5	28.9
Steam Railroads	57.5	23.5
Electric and Street Railways	52.9	21.8
Telegraph and Telephone	25.4	10.2
Post	24.8	31.6
Teamsters and Chauffeurs	11.9	7.0
Construction of Streets	8.3	2.4

The very substantial growth of membership among telegraph and telephone workers came from the fact that the railroad telegraphers' membership was in 1920 three times that of 1910; whereas the membership of the commercial telegraphers' union was insignificant in both years. Another important factor in this situation was the establishment, a few years after 1910, of a union among women telephone operators. The figures for the extent of organization among teamsters and chauffeurs are probably underestimates in both census years because of the great practical difficulties involved in separating this group into the employers and wage earners and in calculating the percentage organized of wage earners alone.

Labor organization in professional service is restricted almost completely to the theatre and to musicians, although there has recently grown up a small union of engineering draftsmen. Among the clerical workers the principal source of growth since 1910 is the rapid spread of organization among the railway clerks. Unionism in domestic and personal service is in 1920 as in 1910 limited to fair organization among barbers and waiters and to exceedingly slim organization among laundry workers.

All of these figures naturally raise interesting questions as to their significance in estimating the relative strength of labor organization in various occupations and industries. High and low percentages of organization are not necessarily synonymous with strength and weakness, and need, in fact, to be interpreted with some reference to the nature of the industry in which the unions operate and to the constitution of the particular union. In general, percentages of organization by industry are misleading unless the fact that the large bulk of American unions are occupational or trade unions is taken into consideration. Because of this highly significant characteristic, union membership in any industry does not represent the membership of a single union claiming jurisdiction over all the employees in that industry, but it is really an aggregate of the memberships of many unions, some limiting their jurisdiction to the workers in a single skilled craft and others admitting a more diversified lot of semi-skilled and unskilled workers. The only outstanding exceptions to this rule are the mining and clothing unions, which are essentially industrial unions.

The unions of skilled craft workers are, also, the older and stronger organizations and their membership is on the whole less subject to fluctuation. The unions of semi-skilled and unskilled workers are more recently organized, weaker and more sensitive to the strains imposed by industrial depression. When, accordingly, these diverse classes of workers are combined into one industrial category, the real strength of the skilled unions is, to a degree, concealed in the gross results. This is particularly true of the building trades and steam railroad industry, where the backbone of unionism has for a long time been the relatively few organizations of skilled craftsmen. The following table shows clearly the divergence between the extent of

TABLE 17.—PER CENT OF ORGANIZATION AMONG SELECTED OCCUPATIONS IN THE BUILDING TRADES
1920 AND 1910

Occupation	Per Cent Organized	
	1920	1910
Brick and Stone Masons	50.0	39.1
Carpenters and Joiners	40.5	20.8
Painters, etc	29.1	17.6
Plasterers	46.6	32.0
Plumbers and Gas Fitters	33.5	20.7

organization for the building trades as a whole and among a few skilled crafts. Thus in 1920, when all employees in the building trades were just about one-fourth organized, the bricklayers, carpenters and plasterers were about 50 per cent, and the plumbers more than one-third organized. The same disparities existed in 1910. At that time the whole industry was one-sixth organized, but the bricklayers and plasterers were about one-third organized.

On the steam railroads, likewise, even the very high percentage of organization for the industry as a whole, 56.7 per cent, was exceeded by the percentages of organization for railway conductors, locomotive engineers, and locomotive firemen.[1] Census statistics for the groups of locomotive firemen and enginemen are unfortunately not reliable, because of the confusion in enumeration between stationary and locomotive firemen and engineers. This confusion led to an overestimate in the number of locomotive engineers as compared with the locomotive firemen and probably a gross over-

[1] Tables VIII and IX.

estimate of both groups.[1] Union membership statistics are likewise defective, since the Brotherhood of Locomotive Firemen, which because of its insurance features retains as members firemen who have become engineers and who are, consequently, also members of the engineers' union, was unable to separate its membership into engineers and firemen. The figures as they now stand contain some double counting in the membership of the firemen's union. It is known, however, that both the engineers and firemen were well over 75 per cent organized in 1920. Railway conductors are likewise nearly 100 per cent organized, although the statistics indicate an organization of only 72 per cent, less than in 1910. The discrepancy between 1910 and 1920 is due in large part to the failure of the Brotherhood of Railroad Trainmen to report the number of its members who were railway conductors. In 1910 this number amounted to 13,000; union membership for 1920 is, consequently, understated. Furthermore, the census reports a larger number of railway conductors than does the Interstate Commerce Commission.[2] According to this agency the average number of conductors on class I railroads in the year ending December 31, 1920 was 58,321, whereas the census figure for early January, 1920 is 74,539. It is possible that a portion of this difference may be due to the reporting by the census of electric railway conductors as working on steam railroads.[3]

Another factor that should be taken into account in judging the strength of the labor movement in the United States is the size and infinite variety of the country. The enormous expense of conducting organization campaigns and of maintaining a staff of organizers all over the country, as well as the inherent difficulty of organizing a thin and scattered industrial population has concentrated trade unions, in many industries, in the large industrial cities. There is, moreover, considerable evidence, although the supporting data are not available, that labor organization is much more widespread in certain sections of the country than in others.

[1] The Census of Occupations reports for 1920, 91,345 locomotive firemen and 109,899 locomotive engineers. The Interstate Commerce Commission, however (*Annual Report on Statistics of Railways in the United States*, 1920, pp. ix, xix, xx), reports the average number of locomotive engineers, on class I railroads, in the year ending December 31, 1920, to be 67,887 and the average number of locomotive firemen, 69,935.

[2] *Annual Report on Statistics of Railways in the United States*, 1920, p. 20.

[3] Census of Occupations, 1920, p. 16.

The South as a whole, for example, even in its industrial centers is very thinly organized, if at all; whereas the industrial East would probably show a high percentage of organization. The almost complete absence of trade unions in the textile industry in the South brings down the percentage of organization for the textile industry as a whole, although some of its centers in New England are tolerably well organized. Equally interesting comparisons could be made for other industries and for other sections of the country. But the unions are either unwilling or unable to submit a detailed geographical distribution of their membership.

Two interesting samples, which throw some light on these phenomena, have been collected for the occupations of bricklaying and printing. In the printing trade the largest source of union membership is the newspaper office; whereas the union is weaker in the book and jobbing trade and probably has a very light membership among compositors in small towns, where there are a considerable number of one-man shops. In 1920, compositors, linotypers and typesetters in the United States were 46.4 per cent organized. The next table shows for 1920 the number of compositors in a list of selected cities, the membership of the Typographical Union in those cities and the percentage of organization. Except where membership was affected by peculiar circumstances,

TABLE 18.—PER CENT OF ORGANIZATION AMONG COMPOSITORS, LINOTYPERS AND TYPESETTERS IN SELECTED CITIES
1920

City	Number of Compositors, Linotypers and Typesetters[a]	Membership of Union[b]	Per Cent Organized
New York	21,429	9,044	42.2
Chicago	10,907	5,119	46.9
Philadelphia	5,708	1,606	28.1
St. Louis	2,205	1,323	60.0
San Francisco	1,457	1,257	86.2
Baltimore	1,886	898	47.6
Cleveland	1,741	1,033	59.3
Boston	2,713	2,098	77.3

[a] Census of Occupations, 1920.
[b] From central office of the International Typographical Union.

the extent of organization was higher than in the whole country. Thus in St. Louis, San Francisco, Cleveland and Boston it was considerably higher. Philadelphia, which has the lowest per cent of organization, is notoriously low in the scale of organization in all industries. Percentages are lowered in New York and Chicago by lack of control over book and job printing establishments in particular and over the small printing shops in general; while in Baltimore the union has not recovered from the weakening effect of the strike for the 44-hour week of a few years ago, in which it lost many members.

Similar data for the bricklaying trade, contained in this next tabulation, is even more convincing on this point. In every large city the percentage of organization was considerably greater than the 50 per cent for the entire United States. Obvious discrepancies

TABLE 19. — PER CENT OF ORGANIZATION AMONG BRICK AND STONE MASONS IN SELECTED CITIES
1920

City	Number of Brick and Stone Masons[a]	Membership of Union[b]	Per Cent Organized
Chicago	5,303	4,229	79.7
Baltimore	1,194	927	77.6
Boston	1,274	1,220	95.8
Cleveland	2,351	1,866	79.4
New York	9,985	5,925	59.3
Philadelphia	3,818	2,188	57.3
Pittsburgh	1,159	1,273	....

[a] Census of Occupations, 1920.

[b] Average monthly membership for year ended June 30, 1920. *First Biennial and 53d Report of the President, Secretary, and Official Auditor*, Bricklayers, Masons and Plasterers' Union, 1920.

in the table, such as the excess in the membership of the union in Pittsburgh over the number of masons in the city, may be due to the fact that the census figures are as of early January while the union statistics are the average for the fiscal year. The appreciably lower percentage of organization in New York City may be explained by the lack of union control over the many small building operations in the outlying areas of the city.

More than three years have elapsed since the taking of the census of occupations of 1920. It is known that in this period trade unions lost heavily in membership. The trend in the size of the working population during the same period is still a matter of speculation. Aggregate statistics of the 1923 census of manufactures are not available at this writing. What evidence there is would seem to indicate a smaller number of employees in manufacturing industries in 1923 than in 1920. The statistics of the Interstate Commerce Commission show fewer persons employed on steam railroads during 1923 than during 1920. How large was the total decline, if any, in the number of employees of the country in these last years cannot be estimated. All things considered, however, it is probable that the extent of organization for all industry was considerably greater in 1923 than in the years immediately before and after the declaration of the World War; that for manufacturing industries it is substantially less in 1923 than in 1920; that in transportation and mining the drop from 1920 to 1923 is not so great as in manufacturing industries; and that in the building trades, the drop in these last years was slight and organization in that industry in 1923 stood little, if at all, below 1920.

Any forecast of the trend of union organization in the future must reckon with two conditions that are comparatively strange in the American industrial situation. The first of these is legislation restricting immigration into the United States. The immigration law of 1924 establishes immigrant quotas which may reduce enormously the flow of immigrant labor into the country. The effect of this restrictive measure has already been noticed as one of the causes of the growth of labor organization in the clothing industry. It may be expected to exert the same kind of influence in other industries as well. The second factor is not so tangible and has to do with the probable influence in the future of the impetus given the movement by large gains made since 1915. Already, even in the cases where heavy losses have been registered since 1920, there is some evidence of the consolidation by labor organizations of at least a portion of their advances. How potent a force this impetus is, it is hazardous to guess; but it is easy to underestimate the influence of intangible social forces of this kind.

CHAPTER V

WOMEN IN TRADE UNIONS IN 1920 AND 1910

Women in the American labor movement have been subjected to many inquiries, but the statistical yield of these inquiries has been very meager indeed. Discussion has turned largely on the problem of organizing women into trade unions, on the general assumption, supported by stray facts, that women in industry were hardly organized at all. A continuous series of the membership of women in labor organizations is impossible to collect and where collected would be impaired by a high percentage of inaccuracy. This phase of the study of women in trade unions was accordingly limited to the statistics of female membership in the years 1920 and 1910. The data for 1910 were taken from an earlier study by the present author in which a careful collection was made of the female membership of all unions known to have women members. The figures for 1920 were collected through correspondence with the central offices of the various unions and were checked for their reasonableness.[1] Many labor organizations are now beginning to keep separate records of their men and women members. It should be easier in the future to assemble annual statistics of female membership in the United States.

Female membership, the next table shows, is more than quintupled in the decade from 1910 to 1920. The sources of the gain were many. All organizations but two, the musicians and the brewery workers, had a larger membership in the latter year. Three important new organizations, which were not in existence in 1910, the Amalgamated Clothing Workers, the Amalgamated Textile Workers, and the telephone operators' branch of the Electrical Workers, contributed practically 100,000 members, or nearly one-fourth of the total rise. Another organization, the Railway

[1] Figures for 1920 are taken from the Appendix, Table V; for 1910 from *Quarterly Journal of Economics*, May, 1916, p. 602, Table I.

Clerks, whose female membership in 1910 was negligible, was responsible for 35,000 more in 1920. In both years the membership of the clothing unions was the dominating item. The International Ladies' Garment Workers and the United Garment Workers had, in 1910, 40 per cent of the total; and in 1920 these same organizations, together with the Amalgamated Clothing Workers, had 42 per cent. By 1920, however, the shoe, textile, railway clerks,

TABLE 20.—FEMALE MEMBERSHIP OF AMERICAN UNIONS 1910 AND 1920

Name of Union	Membership	
	1910	1920
Actors	.....	3,900
Bookbinders	3,771	9,200
Boot and Shoe Workers	5,500	15,000
Box Makers	400	.....
Brewery Workers	550	200
Cigar Makers	4,000	7,000
Cloth Hat and Cap Makers	200	2,500
Clothing Workers, Amalgamated	.....	70,000
Electrical Workers	.....	14,000
Fur Workers	.....	3,600
Garment Workers, United	20,000	32,000
Glove Workers	365	700
Hatters	.....	2,000
Hotel Employees	2,015	5,600
I. W. W. (Chicago)	2,000	.....
I. W. W. (Detroit)	345	.....
Ladies' Garment Workers	11,122	67,700
Laundry Workers	2,000	6,200
Leather Goods Workers, Fancy	.....	200
Leather Workers	.....	3,000
Machinists	.....	500
Meat Cutters	.....	5,400
Musical and Theatrical Union	150	.....
Musicians	4,000	2,800
Paper Makers	24	.....
Paper Mill Workers	250	.....
Photo Engravers	3	.....
Post Office Clerks, Nat'l Fed	70	3,000
Post Office Clerks, United	500	2,600
Potters, Operative	100	1,500

TABLE 20. — FEMALE MEMBERSHIP OF AMERICAN UNIONS — *Continued*

Name of Union	Membership	
	1910	1920
Powder Workers	100	.....
Printing Pressmen	1,500	1,500
Pulp and Paper Mill Workers	.....	1,000
Railroad Telegraphers	960	2,500
Railway Clerks	62	35,000
Retail Clerks	2,100	2,900
Shoe Workers' Protective	.....	8,000
Shoe Workers, United	300	13,000
Tailors	800	2,000
Teachers, American Fed. of	.....	5,200
Textile Workers, Amalgamated	.....	15,000
Textile Workers, United	5,955	40,000
Tobacco Workers	2,460	6,500
Travelers' Goods Workers	25	.....
Typographical Union	621	2,200
Vaudeville Artists	.....	3,500
Weavers, Cloth	2,500	.....
White Rats	2,000	.....
Total	76,748	396,900

and electrical workers' unions had risen to a place of importance, with a combined membership of more than one-third of the total. Most of the unions dropped a large part of their female, as well as their male, membership during the years following 1920. The textile unions and the railway clerks were particularly heavy losers. Any estimate of the total loss between 1920 and 1923 can be little more than a guess; but it is judged that it was not much more than 100,000. A considerable part of this loss, moreover, is probably ascribable to the exodus from industry of the many women who found employment in industry during the war.

The course of the labor movement among women in this country is unintelligible without some conception of the number of women who work and the nature of the work they do. Women have, of course, always constituted a relatively small part of the gainfully occupied portion of the country's population. Both in 1910 and in 1920 women represented just about one-fifth of the total number of persons, who in the United States worked for an income and were, therefore, counted in the occupation census. While the number of women who work is small in absolute magnitude, it has since 1880 increased at a much more rapid rate than the total working population. Their rate of increases, in comparison with that of all gainfully occupied, is shown in the accompanying table.[1] While the total working population rose from

Year	Per Cent	
	Females Gainfully Occupied to Female Population 10 Years of Age and Over	Total Gainfully Occupied to Total Population 10 Years of Age and Over
1920	21.1	50.3
1910	23.4	53.3
1900	18.8	50.2
1890	17.4	49.2
1880	14.7	47.3

47.3 to 50.3 per cent of the population 10 years of age and over, the female working population rose from 14.7 to 21.1; and the male gainfully employed moved from 78.7 in 1880 to 78.2 per cent in 1920. The female working population, like the male and total, also apparently slackened in its rate of increase in the decade from 1910 to 1920 and constituted in the latter year a smaller percentage of the entire female population 10 years of age and over than in 1910.

Like the total working population, also, the number of women workers decreased most markedly in agriculture and domestic and personal service. The relative position of the groups of gainfully employed women in 1910 and 1920 in the general divisions of industry is presented in the next table.

Thus in agriculture and in domestic and personal service there were large absolute and relative declines. The substantial gains took place in trade, professional service and in clerical occupations. Manufacturing and mechanical industries hardly moved.

[1] Taken from Table I, Census of Occupations, 1920, p. 33.

TABLE 21. — WOMEN 10 YEARS OF AGE AND OVER ENGAGED IN GAINFUL OCCUPATIONS, DISTRIBUTED BY GENERAL DIVISIONS OF OCCUPATIONS[a]
1920 AND 1910

General Division of Occupations	1920		1910	
	Number	Per Cent Distribution	Number	Per Cent Distribution
All Occupations	8,549,511	100.0	8,075,772	100.0
Agriculture, Forestry, Animal Husbandry	1,084,128	12.7	1,807,501	22.4
Extraction of Minerals	2,864	[b]	1,094	[b]
Manufacturing and Mechanical Industries	1,930,341	22.6	1,820,570	22.5
Transportation	213,054	2.5	106,625	1.3
Trade	667,792	7.8	468,088	5.8
Public Service	21,794	0.3	13,558	0.2
Professional Service	1,016,498	11.9	733,891	9.1
Domestic and Personal Service	2,186,924	25.6	2,531,221	31.3
Clerical Occupations	1,426,116	16.7	593,224	7.3

[a] Census of Occupations, 1920, p. 34.
[b] Less than one-tenth of one per cent.

Obviously the working population of women is concentrated in industrial categories different from those in which men cluster. There are some groups that tend to become predominantly female and others predominantly male. The salient facts regarding this distribution of the sexes are shown in the next table for the last two census years. More than half of the gainfully employed women in 1920 worked in the professional, domestic and personal services, and clerical occupations. And in two of these occupational divisions, professional service and clerical occupations, women are gradually becoming as numerous as men. The rise in importance of women in professional service is attributable mainly to very great increases from 1910 to 1920 in the number of women teachers and trained nurses. The first group increased 160,000 and the second 40,000; whereas the whole increase in the number of women in professional service in the same period was, roughly, 250,000. Domestic and

TABLE 22.—PER CENT DISTRIBUTION BY SEX OF PERSONS 10 YEARS OF AGE AND OVER IN EACH GENERAL DIVISION OF OCCUPATIONS[a] 1920 AND 1910

General Division of Occupations	1920		1910	
	Male	Female	Male	Female
All Occupations	79.5	20.5	78.8	21.2
Agriculture, Forestry, Animal Husbandry	90.1	9.9	85.7	14.3
Extraction of Minerals	99.7	0.3	99.9	0.1
Manufacturing and Mechanical Industries	84.9	15.1	82.9	17.1
Transportation	93.0	7.0	96.0	4.0
Trade	84.3	15.7	87.1	12.9
Public Service	97.2	2.8	97.0	3.0
Professional Service	52.6	47.4	56.7	43.3
Domestic and Personal Service	35.8	64.2	32.9	67.1
Clerical Occupations	54.4	45.6	65.8	34.2

[a] Census of Occupations, 1920, p. 34.

personal service was predominantly female in 1920 as it was in 1910, but there was a distinct recession as between the two census years, there being in 1920, roughly, 350,000 less women employed in this group than ten years before. In so far as the census figures are correct, this very great fall was due to losses of 140,000 for "laundresses (not in laundry)," 30,000 for "boarding-house keepers," and 300,000 for "servants."

These statistics on women in industry are open to much the same comment as has already been made concerning the movement of the total gainfully occupied population of the country. The conclusion that there has been a drop in the rate with which women enter gainful occupations must be accepted with caution and with some further inquiry into the sources of gain and loss between 1910 and 1920. During the intercensal period the female population 10 years of age and over increased more than 15 per cent and the number of gainfully employed women about 6 per cent. A table, similar to one included in an earlier chapter, indicating the percentage change in the number of gainfully employed women in groups in which they work in substantial numbers, is here presented.

TABLE 23.—CHANGES IN NUMBER OF GAINFULLY EMPLOYED WOMEN
1910 TO 1920

General Division of Occupations	Per Cent Change
Manufacturing Industries	6.4
Transportation	100.0
Trade	43.4
Professional Service	38.5
Domestic and Personal Service	– 13.6
Clerical	141.3
Agriculture	– 40.0

All groups but agriculture, domestic and personal service, and manufacturing industries, had most striking increases in this intercensal period. The reasons for the drop in domestic and personal service have just been cited. The movement in the number of agricultural women workers is confused by factors affecting the nature of the census count. On this matter the census makes the following statement:[1] "In the case of women . . . the great decrease from 1910 to 1920 in the proportion engaged in gainful occupations may be in part apparent only and due to an over-enumeration in 1910. . . . The number of females returned by the Thirteenth Census enumerators as engaged in gainful occupations was excessive, especially as to the number returned as engaged in agricultural pursuits. The increase from 1900 to 1910 in the number of females returned as agricultural laborers was particularly striking—an increase of 129.5 per cent, as compared with an increase of only 23.3 per cent from 1890 to 1900. . . . It is believed that the Thirteenth Census enumerators, working under more liberal instructions and construing these instructions more loosely, returned as gainfully occupied females who would not have been so returned by the Fourteenth Census enumerators." The slight relative rise in the number of women employed in manufacturing industries is equally puzzling and may, perhaps, also be explained by this statement from the census. The drop in the number of women in the employer and self-employed class, composed largely

[1] Census of Occupations, 1920, pp. 23, 24.

of such groups as milliners, tailoresses, and in the employee class of the clothing industry is hardly to have been expected and would appear to be due more to changes in the methods of enumeration than to an actual retardation of the rate of entry of women into manufacturing industries.

The female working population of the country is in the next table distributed among the classes of employers and self-employed, salaried persons, and wage earners, in accordance with the principles of classification already discussed in Chapter III. It is doubtful whether the statistics for women, in this regard, are as reliable as those for the total population. They are here presented for what they are worth. Of the total number of women gainfully engaged in industry, 70 per cent were in 1920 wage earners

TABLE 24.—CLASSIFICATION OF WOMEN INTO EMPLOYER, SALARIED AND WAGE-EARNING CLASSES
1920 AND 1910

	Number of Women	
	1920	1910
Employers and Self-Employed	1,790,370	2,542,008
Salaried (Supervisory and Professional)	710,386	516,402
Wage Earners (Manual and Clerical)	6,047,922	5,014,520

and 62 per cent were in 1910 wage earners. The material drop in the employer and self-employed group from 1910 to 1920 is due to a fall of 600,000 in agriculture and a loss of 200,000 in manufacturing industries, to which reference has already been made. The decrease in agriculture is largely a result of the change in the methods of enumeration and there is some probability that the changes in manufacturing are due, in a measure also, to the same factors.

The number of women in trade unions is relatively as well as absolutely small. When female membership is compared with the number of women wage earners in all industry, as well as in the various classifications of industry, the extent of trade unionism is found to run in every case substantially below that for men. A conspectus of the position of unionism among women in the major divisions of industry is submitted in this next tabulation. It shows in general that while all wage earners were in 1920 about one-fifth

TABLE 25. — PER CENT OF ORGANIZATION AMONG FEMALE WAGE EARNERS IN MAJOR DIVISIONS OF INDUSTRY 1920 AND 1910

Division of Industry	Per Cent Organized	
	1920	1910
Total Wage Earners (except agriculture)	6.6	1.5
Manufacturing Industries	18.3	5.2
Transportation	6.5	0.9
Trade	0.5	0.5
Clerical Occupations	2.7	0.1
Domestic Service	0.6	0.1
Professional Service	1.5	0.8

organized, women, even excluding from the calculation the female agricultural wage earners, were in the same year only one-fifteenth organized. All of the groups but one, trade, showed some increase in organization in the decade, but in manufacturing alone does the movement assume substantial proportions. In the comparison, however, between the strength of unionism among men and women, it must not be overlooked that mining and building, two strongholds of labor organization among men, are industries in which women play no part. Furthermore, women happen to be working, in the largest proportions, precisely in those occupational divisions which are notoriously weak in labor organization even among men. In 1920 more than 60 per cent of the women gainfully engaged in industry were employed in trade, professional service, domestic and personal service, and clerical occupations; but in that same year less than 25 per cent of the male working population of the country was employed in the same groups.

In only a few of the manufacturing industries did women achieve fairly strong organization by 1920. The greatest gain from 1910 to 1920 and also the highest level attained in the latter year was reached in the clothing industry, where almost half of the women employees were in 1920 members of labor organizations. Large advances were made also in the leather industry, where unionism was much stronger in 1920 among both the shoe and miscellaneous leather branches of the industry. The percentage of organization in the liquor industry must be used carefully, first because there is some question as to the accuracy of the figures and second because there were credited to the industry in 1920 only 930 women employees, of whom 200 were organized. Unionism in the clay, glass and stone industries was localized entirely in potteries, where organization among women made great strides from 1910 to 1920. The very slight percentage of organization for the group of food industries in 1920, 5.6, conceals a substantial organization of 42.6 per cent among women packing and slaughter-house employees. Increase in the membership of the bookbinders' union explains the doubling of the percentage of organization in the printing and publishing industry. Since 1920 the unions in the slaughter and

TABLE 26.—PER CENT OF ORGANIZATION AMONG FEMALE WAGE EARNERS IN MANUFACTURING INDUSTRIES
1920 AND 1910

Division of Industry	Per Cent Organized	
	1920	1910
All Manufacturing	18.3	5.2
Chemical and Allied	....	0.6
Clay, Glass and Stone	8.5	0.8
Clothing	46.0	11.2
Food	5.6	....
Iron and Steel	0.7	....
Leather	42.6	8.0
Liquor and Beverage	21.5	24.4
Lumber	....	2.1
Metal (except Iron and Steel)	....	....
Paper and Pulp	1.3	0.8
Printing and Publishing	25.0	11.6
Textile	11.5	2.6
Cigar and Tobacco	13.5	8.0

packing-house and textile industries have had particularly heavy losses in membership. Organization among women in those industries would therefore be not much greater than it was in 1910. For the rest, except clothing, which retains most of its strength, the case is doubtful, but they are probably all on a higher level of organization now than they were before the war.

Organization in the transportation industry is restricted to the telegraph and telephone industry. In this industry the railroad telegraphers' union and the telephone operators' branch of the electrical workers' union are responsible for an organization of 7 per cent.

The type of skilled craft union which is so prevalent among men and which plays so dominant a rôle in the American labor movement is practically non-existent among women. The nearest approach to it is to be found in the unions of professional workers, like actors, musicians, and teachers. Except in the case of actresses, who are now highly organized, unionism is very weak indeed. The statistics for teachers are in all probability an underestimate because they exclude the membership of independent teachers' unions of which there are a number in the country. But the extent of organization among women teachers would, even in the event of the inclusion of the independent membership, not be high.

Among women, as well as among men, there is likely to be a concentration of labor organization in the large cities and in certain sections of the country, particularly the East. A little light is thrown on this question in a survey, made in 1922 by the Division of Women in Industry of the New York State Department of Labor, of the extent of trade unionism among gainfully employed women in cities over 50,000 in population in New York State. A table from this survey is reproduced here. It shows that more than one-fourth of the total female union membership of the country is found in New York State. Without making allowance for the fact that computing the percentage of organization among women "wage earners" would yield a higher figure than that for organization among women gainfully employed in industry, the percentage in trade unions for this group is nevertheless about twice as large as in the whole country.

TAALE 27.—NUMBER AND PERCENTAGE OF WOMEN TRADE UNION MEMBERS IN NEW YORK STATE IN CITIES OVER 50,000[a]
1920

Cities Over 50,000	Number Women Gainfully Employed	Number Women in Trade Unions	Percentage in Trade Unions
Total	871,503	113,354	13.0
Greater New York	693,096	96,162	14.3
Albany	15,547	1,043	6.7
Binghamton	9,341	144	1.5
Buffalo	50,218	3,732	7.4
Niagara Falls	3,887	56	1.4
Rochester	37,725	9,515	25.2
Schenectady	8,331	515	6.2
Syracuse	18,814	481	2.6
Troy	12,039	1,213	10.1
Utica	12,261	469	3.8
Yonkers	11,244	24	0.2

[a] Reprinted from "Women Who Work," New York State Department of Labor, *Special Bulletin, No. 110,* April, 1922, p. 28.

These figures for New York State could not easily be duplicated elsewhere because of the leading position that the clothing industry occupies in that state. And it is the clothing industry which in 1920 topped all other industries in the extent of organization among women. Thus in the preceding table Greater New York and Rochester contributed more than 105,000 of the total of 113,354 women members of trade unions. In Rochester more than 70 per cent of the 9,500 union members belonged to unions in the garment trades, and in Greater New York the percentage was 65. In Greater New York alone is there a noticeable sprinkling of union membership among other industries as well. But here, except for a substantial membership in the theatre and music group, the clothing and textile groups absorb 75,000 of the total 96,000 members in the whole city.[1]

[1] *Ibid,* p. 31.

APPENDIX

TABLE I. — MEMBERSHIP OF

(00's

UNLESS OTHERWISE INDICATED, THE DATA CONTAINED IN THIS TABLE WERE OBTAINED
WERE OBTAINED FROM THE PROCEEDINGS OF THE UNION OR BY

	Name of Union	1897	1898	1899	1900	1901	1902	1903	1904	1905	1906	1907
	Mining and Quarrying											
1	Coal Hoisting Engineers........	....	....	5[a]	7[a]	10[a]	8[a]	9[a]	•	....	....	....
2	Mine Managers and Assts......	....	....	....	....	....	4[a]	4[a]	4[a]	4[a]	4[a]	•
3	Mine, Mill and Smelter Workers.	....	....	....	....	....	....	....	....	....	....	....
4	Mine Workers, United.........	*97*[a]	*329*[a]	*618*[a]	*1155*[a]	*1980*[a]	*1753*[a]	*2472*[a]	*2510*[a]	*2650*[a]	*2307*[a]	*2607*[a]
5	Mineral Mine Workers.........	28[a]	7[a]	6[a]	5[a]	4[a]	3[a]	7[a]	[b]	....	....	....
6	Miners, Western Federation....	*80*	*100*	*120*	*140*	*177*	*196*	*283*	*241*	*263*	*286*	*443*
7	Quarry Workers..............	....	....	....	....	....	....	12[a]	26[a]	36[a]	38[a]	41[a]
8	Quarrymen...................	4[a]	4[a]	[b]	....	....	....	....	....	....	....	....
9	Slate Workers................	....	....	....	....	....	....	8[a]	8[a]	9[a]	18[a]	30[a]
	Total in Group.............	209	440	749	1307	2171	1964	2795	2789	2962	2653	3120
	Building Trades											
1	Asbestos Workers.............	....	....	....	....	....	....	....	7[a]	3[a]	5[a]	5[a]
2	Bricklayers and Masons........	*233*	*262*	*267*	*334*	*346*	*439*	*462*	*563*	*548*	*538*	*641*
3	Bridge and Iron Workers.......	....	....	....	....	60[a]	110[c]	160[a]	115[a]	*102*[a]	*98*[a]	*116*[a]
4	Building Employees...........	....	....	....	....	....	....	....	8[a]	[b]	....	....
5	Building Laborers............	....	....	....	....	....	....	....	....	....	....	....
6	Carpenters, Amal.............	16[a]	16[a]	18[a]	20[a]	26[a]	32[a]	45[a]	50[a]	48[a]	43[a]	58[a]
7	Carpenters, United...........	*282*[a]	*315*[a]	*500*[a,c]	*684*[a]	*871*[a]	*1225*[a]	*1672*[a]	*1612*[a]	*1612*[a]	*1702*[a]	*1743*[a,e]
8	Cement Workers..............	....	....	....	....	....	....	55[a]	44[a]	36[a]	42[a]	58[a]
9	Compressed Air Workers.......	....	....	....	....	....	....	....	12[a]	12[a]	13[a]	13[a]
10	Electrical Workers (A. F. of L.)..	17[a]	20[a]	20[a]	48[a]	73[a]	115[a]	183[a]	210[a]	210[a]	210[a]	302[a]
11	Electrical Workers............	....	....	....	....	....	....	....	....	....	....	....
12	Elevator Constructors.........	....	....	....	....	*9*	*12*	21[a]	22[a]	22[a]	22[a]	23[a]
13	Hod Carriers.................	....	....	....	....	....	....	*82*[a]	*120*[a]	*56*[a]	*92*[a]	*102*[a]
14	Lathers, Wood and Metal......	....	....	....	6[a]	14[a]	23[a]	*33*[a]	*39*[a]	*36*[a]	*44*[a]	*55*[a]
15	Marble Workers..............	....	....	....	....	....	5[a]	12[a]	6[a]	19[a]	17[a]	20[a]
16	Painters.....................	50[a]	43[a]	45[a]	280[a]	280[a]	348[a]	536[a]	607[a]	542[a]	555[a]	624[a]
17	Plasterers...................	*20*	*18*	*40*[c]	*63*	*83*[c]	*105*	*114*[c]	*124*	*134*[c]	*145*	*167*
18	Plumbers.....................	40[a]	40[a]	40[a]	45[a]	87[a]	128[a]	152[a]	165[a]	150[a]	150[a]	160[a]
19	Roofers, Composition..........	....	....	....	....	....	....	....	*5*	*7*	*10*	10[a]
20	Roofers, Slate and Tile........	....	....	....	....	....	....	5[a]	7[a]	6[a]	5[a]	6[a]
21	Sheet Metal Workers..........	*10*	*12*	15[a]	29[a]	45[a]	66[a]	126[a]	153[a]	130[a]	129[a]	153[a]
22	Steam Fitters................	*5*	*10*	20[a]	18[a]	15[a]	15[a]	*20*	*30*	*40*	54[a]	55[a]
23	Tile Layers..................	....	2[a]	3[a]	4[a]	7[a]	11[a]	14[a]	17[a]	14[a]	19[a]	21[a]
	Total in Group.............	673	738	968	1531	1916	2634	3692	3916	3727	3893	4332
	Textile											
1	Cloth Weavers...............	....	....	....	....	....	....	....	....	....	....	....
2	Elastic Goring Weavers........	3[a]	3[a]	3[a]	3[a]	2[a]	2[a]	1[a]	1[a]	1[a]	1[a]	1[a]
3	Lace Operatives..............	2[a]	3[a]	3[a]	4[a]	4[a]	5[a]	5[a]	6[a]	7[a]	8[a]	8[a]
4	Loomfixers..................	*25*	*30*	*20*	*15*	*10*	*8*	*7*	*7*	*7*	*8*	*8*
5	Machine Textile Printers.......	....	....	....	....	....	....	4[a]	4[a]	4[a]	4[a]	*4*
6	Silk Workers.................	....	....	....	....	....	....	....	....	....	....	....
7	Spinners.....................	24[a]	24[a]	21[a]	24[a]	27[a]	26[a]	25[a]	25[a]	22[a]	22[a]	22[a]
8	Textile Workers, Amal.........	....	....	....	....	....	....	....	....	....	....	....
9	Textile Workers, United........	27[a]	25[a]	22[a]	34[a]	27[a]	106[a]	150[a]	105[a]	100[a]	100[a]	114[a]
10	Wool Sorters and Graders......	....	....	....	....	....	....	....	....	....	....	....
	Total in Group.............	81	85	69	80	70	147	192	148	141	143	157

AMERICAN TRADE UNIONS, 1897–1923

omitted)

FROM THE REPORTS OF THE AMERICAN FEDERATION OF LABOR. FIGURES IN ITALICS CORRESPONDENCE WITH THE CENTRAL OFFICE OF THE UNION.

1908	1909	1910	1911	1912	1913	1914	1915	1916	1917	1918	1919	1920	1921	1922	1923	
....	....	....	....	....	....	....	....	....	....	....	....	....	....	....	....	1
....	....	....	....	....	....	....	....	....	....	....	....	....	....	....	....	2
....	....	....	....	....	....	....	167[a]	161[a]	179[a]	167[a]	178[a]	211[a]	162[a]	46[a]	81[a]	3
2520[a]	*2652*[a]	*2314*[a]	*2563*[a]	*2893*[a]	*3777*[a]	*3390*[a]	3116[a]	3180[a]	3520[a]	4134[a]	3938[a]	3936[a]	4257[a]	3729[a]	4049[a]	4
....	....	....	....	....	....	....	....	....	....	....	....	....	....	....	....	5
305	*353*	*371*	*502*[a]	*492*[a]	*495*[a]	369[a]	....	....	....	....	....	....	....	....	....	6
45[a]	45[a]	50[a]	35[a]	40[a]	40[a]	40[a]	36[a]	35[a]	35[a]	31[a]	30[a]	30[a]	30[a]	30[a]	24[a]	7
....	....	....	....	....	....	....	....	....	....	....	....	....	....	....	....	8
27[a]	21[a]	14[a]	7[a]	4[a]	3[a]	3[a]	3[a]	b	....	....	....	....	....	....	....	9
2897	3071	2749	3107	3429	4315	3802	3322	3376	3734	4332	4146	4177	4449	3805	4154	
8[a]	6[a]	5[a]	8[a]	8[a]	8[a]	10[a]	10[a]	10[a]	10[a]	16[a]	18[a]	22[a]	26[a]	20[a]	20[a]	1
629	*607*	*618*	*758*	*811*	*844*	*825*	*759*	*738*	*785*[a]	*716*[a]	*652*[a]	*736*[a]	*819*[a]	*852*[a]	*1037*[a]	2
104[a]	*96*[a]	*109*[a]	*122*[a]	*109*[a]	*122*[a]	*132*[a]	*123*[a]	*142*[a]	*160*[e]	*186*[a]	*241*[a]	*277*[a]	*224*[a]	*151*[a]	*170*[a]	3
....	....	....	....	....	....	....	....	....	....	....	....	....	....	....	....	4
....	....	64[d]	70[d]	58[d]	84[d]	98[d]	*111*	*80*	b	....	....	....	....	....	....	5
81[a]	73[a]	71[a]	78[a]	91[d]	b	....	....	....	....	....	....	....	....	....	....	6
1785[a]	*1896*[a c]	*2007*[a]	*1941*[a]	*1955*[a]	*2188*[a]	*2122*[a]	*1940*[a]	*2128*[a]	*2472*[a]	*3217*[a]	*3460*[a]	*3719*[a]	*3550*[a]	*3231*[a]	*3147*[a]	7
73[a]	90[a]	90[a]	90[a]	90[a]	90[a]	73[a]	16[a]	b	....	....	....	....	....	....	....	8
13[a]	8[a]	6[a]	6[a]	6[a]	8[a]	10[a]	12[a]	14[a]	16[a]	b	....	....	....	....	....	9
321[a]	138[a]	160[a]	189[a]	196[a]	227[a]	308[a]	362[a]	362[a]	415[a]	544[a]	1312[a]	1392[a]	1420[a]	1420[a]	1420[a]	10
....	....	....	....	220[d]	230[d]	b	....	....	....	....	....	....	....	....	....	11
25[a]	20[a]	21[a]	21[a]	23[a]	26[a]	27[a]	27[a]	28[a]	29[a]	29[a]	30[a]	31[a]	38[a]	38[a]	52[a]	12
92[a]	*77*[a]	*114*[a]	127[a]	125[a]	221[a]	256[a]	319[a]	324[a]	324[a]	367[a]	400[a]	420[a]	460[a]	460[a]	475[a]	13
54[a]	*51*[a]	*58*[a]	*58*[a]	*59*[a]	*65*[a]	*67*[a]	60[a]	60[a]	60[a]	60[a]	60[a]	59[a]	80[a]	80[a]	80[a]	14
22[a]	24[a]	27[a]	28[a]	28[a]	30[a]	41[a]	16[a]	6[a]	10[a]	10[a]	10[a]	12[a]	12[a]	17[a]	23[a]	15
648[a]	596[a]	635[a]	676[a]	685[a]	709[a]	744[a]	753[a]	782[a]	852[a]	845[a]	827[a]	1031[a]	1133[a]	978[a]	928[a]	16
159	145[a]	152[a]	147[a]	157[a]	173[a]	180[a]	183[a]	184[a]	190[a]	190[a]	190[a]	194[a]	239[a]	246[a]	252[a]	17
180[a]	184[a]	200[a]	200[a]	260[a]	290[a]	297[a]	*410*[a]	*450*[a]	*520*[a]	*600*[a]	*600*[a]	*750*[a]	*420*[a]	*490*[a]	*560*[a]	18
10[a]	10[a]	11[a]	*15*[a]	*15*[a]	*16*[a]	*16*[a]	12[a]	12[a]	12[a]	12[a]	10[a]	18[a]	28[a]	30[a]	30[a]	19
6[a]	5[a]	5[a]	5[a]	5[a]	6[a]	6[a]	6[a]	6[a]	6[a]	6[a]	6[a]	b	....	....	....	20
161[a]	160[a]	162[a]	172[a]	166[a]	169[a]	178[a]	178[a]	175[a]	176[a]	183[a]	202[a]	218[a]	242[a]	250[a]	250[a]	21
56[a]	56[a]	56[a]	56[a]	•	....	....	....	....	....	....	....	....	....	....	....	22
19[a]	17[a]	19[a]	21[a]	24[a]	27[a]	30[a]	30[a]	28[a]	28[a]	25[a]	•	....	....	....	....	23
4446	4259	4590	4788	5091	5533	5420	5327	5529	6065	7006	8018	8879	8691	8263	8444	
....	....	*50*	*50*	50[d]	60[d]	50[d]	....	....	....	....	....	....	....	....	....	1
1[a]	1[a]	1[a]	1[a]	1[a]	1[a]	1[a]	1[a]	1[a]	1[a]	1[a]	1[a]	1[a]	1[a]	1[a]	1[a]	2
8[a]	8[a]	8[a]	9[a]	10[a]	11[a]	12[a]	12[a]	11[a]	12[a]	12[a]	9[a]	9[h]	*16*	*16*	*17*	3
8	*9*	*9*	*13*	*16*	*17*	*16*	....	....	....	....	....	....	....	....	....	4
4	*4*	*4*	*4*	*4*	*4*	*4*	....	....	....	....	....	....	....	....	....	5
....	....	....	....	....	....	....	....	....	....	....	*8*	*10*	*14*	*30*	*35*	6
22[a]	22[a]	22[a]	22[a]	22[a]	22[a]	22[a]	22[a]	22[a]	22[a]	22[a]	22[a]	*22*	*22*	*22*	*22*	7
....	....	....	....	....	....	....	....	....	....	....	....	*400*	i	i	i	8
129[a]	100[a]	100[a]	100[a]	109[a]	162[a]	180[a]	189[a]	255[a]	371[a]	459[a]	558[a]	1049[a]	829[a]	300[a]	300[a]	9
....	....	16[d]	14[d]	14[e]	14[e]	14[d]	....	....	....	....	....	....	....	....	....	10
172	144	210	213	226	291	299	224	289	406	494	598	1491	882	369	375	

Table I. — Membership of American

	Name of Union	1897	1898	1899	1900	1901	1902	1903	1904	1905	1906	1907
	Metal, Machinery, and Shipbuilding											
1	Automobile, Aircraft, etc.	....	....	....	....	....	....	....	....	....	....	....
2	Blacksmiths	3[a]	3[a]	5[a]	15[a]	35[a]	43[a]	70[a]	105[a]	100[a]	82[a]	93[a]
3	Boiler Makers and Iron Shipbuilders	*11*[a]	*13*[a]	*32*[a]	*48*[a]	*54*[a]	*72*[a]	*149*[a]	*180*[a]	*138*[a]	*135*[a]	*185*[a]
4	Brass and Metal Workers	7[a]	[b]	....	....	....	....	....	....	....	....	....
5	Carriage Workers	5[a]	5[a]	7[a]	13[a]	25[a]	31[a]	49[a]	55[a]	32[a]	31[a]	31[a]
6	Car Workers	....	....	....	....	10[a]	24[a]	128[a]	102[a]	50[a]	49[a]	50[a]
7	Chain Makers	....	....	....	2[a]	4[a]	6[a]	6[a]	6[a]	6[a]	6[a]	6[a]
8	Chandelier Workers	....	....	....	....	....	....	....	....	....	....	....
9	Coremakers	5[a]	7[a]	10[a]	12[a]	12[a]	12[a]	[b]	....	....	....	....
10	Cutting Die Makers	....	....	....	....	....	....	....	....	3[a]	3[a]	3[a]
11	Diamond Workers	....	....	....	....	....	....	....	....	....	....	....
12	Draftsmen	....	....	....	....	....	....	....	....	....	....	....
13	Engineers, Amal.	*19*	19[a]	18[a]	18[a]	18[a]	19[a]	*29*	*29*	*29*	*31*	*34*
14	Foundry Employees	....	....	....	....	....	....	....	10[a]	10[a]	10[a]	10[a]
15	Furnace Workers	....	....	....	....	14[a]	9[a]	15[a]	15[a]	15[a]	[b]	....
16	Gold Beaters	5[a]	5[a]	5[a]	*4*	*4*	3[a]	3[a]	3[a]	3[a]	3[a]	5
17	Iron, Steel and Tin Workers	*105*[a]	*105*[a]	*110*[a]	*140*[a]	*139*[a]	*145*[a]	*152*[a]	*143*[a]	*109*[a]	*114*[a]	*102*[a]
18	Jewelry Workers	....	....	....	9[a]	9[a]	10[a]	24[a]	24[a]	7[a]	4[a]	6[a]
19	Machinists	140[a]	100[a]	136[a]	225[a]	325[a]	355[a]	483[a]	557[a]	485[a]	500[a]	560[a]
20	Metal Mechanics	6[a]	7[a]	9[a]	22[a]	45[a]	61[a]	113[a]	70[a]	[b]	....	....[a]
21	Metal Polishers	36[a]	42[a]	48[a]	50[a]	56[a]	84[a]	128[a]	128[a]	103[a]	109[a]	100
22	Metal Work, Brotherhood	....	....	....	....	....	....	....	....	....	....	....[a]
23	Metal Work, United	....	....	....	10[a]	21[a]	43[a]	87[a]	96[a]	[b]	....	....
24	Molders	120[a]	120[a]	150[a]	150[a]	150[a]	259[a]	300[a]	300[a]	300[a]	450[a]	500
25	Pattern Makers	10[a]	13[a]	15[a]	22[a]	23[a]	23[a]	29[a]	37[a]	36[a]	40[a]	50[a]
26	Pocket Knife Grinders	....	....	....	....	....	....	....	....	2[a]	3[a]	3[a]
27	Railway Carmen	*13*	*10*	*11*	30[c]	*49*	121[c]	*193*	177[c]	*160*	243[c]	*326*[a]
28	Saw Smiths	....	....	....	....	....	3[a]	3[a]	3[a]	3[a]	3[a]	3
29	Shipwrights	....	....	....	....	....	....	26[a]	34[a]	24[a]	20[a]	19[a]
30	Stove Mounters	7[a]	6[a]	6[a]	9[a]	13[a]	16[a]	16[a]	17[a]	15[a]	15[a]	15[a]
31	Table Knife Grinders	2[a]	2[a]	3[a]	2[a]	2[a]	2[a]	3[a]	3[a]	3[a]	3[a]	3[a]
32	Tack Makers	....	....	....	....	....	....	1[a]	2[a]	2[a]	[b]	....[a]
33	Tin Plate Workers	....	....	17[a]	21[a]	20[a]	21[a]	18[a]	16[a]	14[a]	14[a]	14
34	Tube Workers	....	....	....	....	....	5[a]	15[a]	15[a]	[b]	....	....[a]
35	Watch Case Engravers	....	....	....	5[a]	5[a]	4[a]	4[a]	3[a]	3[a]	2[a]	2
36	Watch Case Makers	....	....	....	....	3[a]	....	[b]	....	....	....	....[a]
37	Wire Drawers	5[a]	3[a]	5[a]	....	....	....	[b]	....	....	....	....
38	Wire Weavers	*2*	*2*	*2*	2[a]	2[a]	2[a]	3[a]	3[a]	3[a]	3[a]	3[a]
	Total in Group	501	462	589	809	1038	1373	2052	2133	1655	1873	2123
	Public Service											
1	Federal Employees	....	....	....	....	....	....	....	....	....	....	....
2	Fire Fighters	....	....	....	....	....	....	....	....	....	....	....
3	Government Employees	....	....	....	....	....	....	....	....	....	....	....
4	Letter Carriers	*111*	112[c]	*113*	*132*	141[c]	*150*	*166*	*169*	*170*	*173*	*205*
5	Letter Carriers, Rural	....	....	....	....	....	....	....	....	....	....	....
6	Post Office Clerks, United	....	....	....	*22*	*35*	*40*	*50*	*65*	*75*	*85*	*100*
7	Post Office Clerks, National	....	....	....	....	....	....	....	....	....	....	9[a]
8	Railway Mail Assn.	....	....	....	....	....	....	....	....	....	....	....
9	Railway Postal Clerks	....	....	....	....	....	....	....	....	....	....	....
10	State, City Employees	....	....	....	....	....	....	....	....	....	....	....
11	Teachers, Amer. Fed. of	....	....	....	....	....	....	....	....	....	....	....
	Total in Group	111	112	113	154	176	190	216	234	245	258	314

Trade Unions, 1897–1923 — *Continued*

1908	1909	1910	1911	1912	1913	1914	1915	1916	1917	1918	1919	1920	1921	1922	1923	
....	....	....	....	....	....	....	*130*	*172*	*195*	*232*	*381*	*454*	[f]	....	....	1
100[a]	100[a]	100[a]	100[a]	93[a]	90[a]	96[a]	85[a]	97[a]	120[a]	183[a]	283[a]	483[a]	500[a]	367[a]	50[a]	2
130[a]	*133*[a]	*161*[a]	199[a]	167[a]	162[a]	167[a]	173[a]	182[a]	312[a]	555[a]	849[a]	1030[a]	845[a]	417[a]	194[a]	3
....	....	....	....	....	....	....	....	....	....	....	....	....	....	....	....	4
15[a]	15[a]	11[a]	20[a]	27[a]	29[a]	35[a]	38[a]	40[a]	42[a]	[e]	....	....	....	....	....	5
44[a]	50[a]	50[a]	46[a]	*74*	105[d]	110[d]	....	....	....	....	....	....	....	....	....	6
6[a]	3[a]	2[a]	[e]	....	....	....	....	....	....	....	....	....	....	....	....	7
....	....	....	....	....	3[d]	4[d]	....	....	....	....	....	....	....	....	....	8
....	....	....	....	....	....	....	....	....	....	....	....	....	....	....	....	9
3[a]	3[a]	3[a]	3[a]	3[a]	3[a]	3[a]	3[a]	2[a]	2[a]	2[a]	2[a]	2[a]	3[a]	3[a]	[b]	10
....	....	*3*	*3*	3[a]	3[a]	3[a]	3[a]	3[a]	4[a]	4[a]	5[a]	6[a]	6[a]	5[a]	5[a]	11
....	....	....	....	....	....	....	....	....	....	....	18[a]	35[a]	22[a]	10[a]	6[a]	12
28	*31*	*38*	*38*	34[d]	*38*	27[d]	*34*	*32*	*30*	*28*	*26*	[b]	....	....	....	13
7[a]	5[a]	7[a]	5[a]	5[a]	5[a]	6[a]	6[a]	8[a]	13[a]	33[a]	54[a]	91[a]	52[a]	40[a]	40[a]	14
....	....	....	....	....	....	....	....	....	....	....	....	....	....	....	....	15
5[a]	[e]	....	....	....	....	....	....	....	....	....	....	....	....	....	....	16
74[a]	*63*[a]	*82*[a]	*43*[a]	*55*[a]	*63*[a]	*65*[a]	65[a]	67[a]	110[a]	161[a]	197[a]	315[a]	254[a]	159[a]	117[a]	17
4[a]	3[a]	4[a]	3[a]	2[a]	[b]	[b]	[b]	53[a]	43[a]	48[a]	51[a]	81[a]	*70*[e]	*70*[e]	*22*[a]	18
621[a]	484[a]	569[a]	671[a]	598[a]	710[a]	754[a]	719[a]	1009[a]	1125[a]	1436[a]	2546[a]	3308[a]	2736[a]	1809[a]	973[a]	19
....	....	....	....	....	....	....	....	....	....	....	....	....	....	....	....	20
100[a]	100[a]	100[a]	100[a]	100[a]	100[a]	100[a]	*110*[a]	*115*[a]	*120*[a]	*135*[a]	*130*[a]	*125*[a]	*95*[a]	*90*[a]	*92*[a]	21
....	*9*	*13*	*14*[e]	*14*[e]	*15*	*17*	....	....	....	....	....	*150*	....	....	*60*	22
....	....	....	....	....	....	....	....	....	....	....	....	....	....	....	....	23
500[a]	500[a]	500[a]	500[a]	500[a]	500[a]	500[a]	500[a]	500[a]	500[a]	500[a]	516[a]	573[a]	585[a]	265[a]	321[a]	24
55[a]	50[a]	52[a]	56[a]	60[a]	65[a]	67[a]	65[a]	65[a]	70[a]	88[a]	90[a]	90[a]	90[a]	80[a]	80[a]	25
3[a]	3[a]	3[a]	3[a]	3[a]	3[a]	3[a]	3[a]	2[a]	[e]	....	....	....	....	....	....	26
251[c]	*175*	228[a]	269[a]	287[a]	280[a]	287[a]	293[a]	308[a]	390[a]	534[a]	1004[a]	1821[a]	2000[a]	1717[a]	1600[a]	27
3[a]	3[a]	3[a]	1[a]	1[a]	1[a]	1[a]	1[a]	1[a]	1[a]	1[a]	1[a]	1[a]	1[a]	1[a]	1[a]	28
16[a]	16[a]	9[a]	9[d]	[b]	....	....	....	....	....	....	....	....	....	....	....	29
14[a]	10[a]	9[a]	11[a]	11[a]	11[a]	11[a]	11[a]	12[a]	17[a]	19[a]	19[a]	19[a]	20[a]	20[a]	18[a]	30
3[a]	2[a]	2[a]	[e]	....	....	....	....	....	....	....	....	....	....	....	....	31
....	....	....	....	....	....	....	....	....	....	....	....	....	....	....	....	32
14[a]	15[a]	8[a]	3[a]	3[a]	[b]	....	....	....	....	....	....	....	....	....	....	33
....	....	....	....	....	....	....	....	....	....	....	....	....	....	....	....	34
2[a]	2[a]	2[a]	2[a]	[e]	....	....	....	....	....	....	....	....	....	....	....	35
....	....	....	....	....	....	....	....	....	....	....	....	....	....	....	....	36
....	....	....	....	....	....	....	....	....	....	....	....	....	....	....	....	37
3[a]	3[a]	4[a]	4[a]	3[a]	3[a]	3[a]	3[a]	3[a]	3[a]	3[a]	3[a]	4[a]	4[a]	4[a]	4[a]	38
2001	1778	1963	2103	2043	2189	2259	2242	2671	3097	3962	6175	8588	7283	5057	3583	
....	....	....	....	....	....	....	....	....	81[a]	109[a]	204[a]	385[a]	330[a]	250[a]	212[a]	1
....	....	....	....	....	....	....	....	....	....	23[a]	154[a]	221[a]	180[a]	161[a]	160[a]	2
....	....	*100*	*100*	80[d]	60[d]	*40*	....	....	....	....	....	....	....	....	....	3
225	*250*	*260*	*271*	*269*	*291*	*322*	*332*	*334*	*328*[a]	*325*[a]	*339*[a]	*224*[a]	*354*[a]	*399*[a]	*409*[a]	4
....	....	....	....	....	....	....	....	....	....	....	....	3[a]	16[a]	10[a]	6[a]	5
150	*180*	*210*	*220*	*230*	*250*	*260*	*280*	*290*	*290*	*240*	*270*	*290*	*310*	*350*	*370*	6
12[a]	13[a]	14[a]	*70*[a]	*90*[a]	*100*[a]	*120*[a]	*140*[a]	*150*[a]	*170*[a]	*210*[a]	*230*[a]	*250*[a]	*270*[a]	*300*[a]	*350*[a]	7
....	....	....	....	....	122[d]	129[d]	*133*	*135*	*134*	*135*[a]	*147*[a]	*148*[a]	*165*[a]	*167*[a]	*169*[a]	8
....	....	....	....	....	....	15[a]	20[a]	27[a]	[b]	....	....	....	....	....	....	9
....	....	....	....	....	39[d]	28[d]	....	....	....	....	....	....	....	....	....	10
....	....	....	....	....	....	....	....	27[a]	21[a]	10[a]	28[a]	93[a]	93[a]	70[a]	46[a]	11
387	443	584	661	669	862	914	905	963	1024	1052	1372	1614	1718	1707	1722	

Table I. — Membership of American

	Name of Union	1897	1898	1899	1900	1901	1902	1903	1904	1905	1906	1907
	Leather											
1	Boot and Shoe Workers........	125[a]	94[a]	43[a]	47[a]	88[a]	146[a]	297[a]	320[a]	320[a]	321[a]	320[a]
2	Boot and Shoe Cutters.........	....	....	....	....	....	....	....	....	....	....	....
3	Leather Goods Workers, Fancy..	....	....	....	....	....	....	....	....	....	....	....
4	Leather Workers on Horse Goods	1[a]	4[a]	10[a]	21[a]	32[a]	42[a]	48[a]	46[a]	40[a]	40[a]	40[a]
5	Leather Workers, Amal.........	....	....	....	....	3[a]	22[a]	36[a]	25[a]	10[a]	10[a]	10[a]
6	Leather Workers, United.......	....	....	....	....	....	....	....	....	....	....	....
7	Shoe Workers' Protective.......	*25*	*25*	*25*	*25*	*25*	*25*	*25*	*25*	*25*	*25*	*25*
8	Shoe Workers, Utd............	....	....	....	....	....	....	....	....	....	....	....
9	Trav. Goods and Leather Nov. Workers....................	*1*	*1*	*2*	3[a]	3[a]	5[a]	16[a]	15[a]	13[a]	9[a]	7[a]
	Total in Group.............	152	124	80	96	151	240	422	431	408	405	402
	Clothing											
1	Cloth, Hat and Cap Makers....	....	....	....	....	....	20[a]	25[a]	29[a]	26[a]	21[a]	23[a]
2	Clothing Workers, Amalgamated	....	....	....	....	....	....	....	....	....	....	....
3	Garment Workers, United......	40[a]	43[a]	42[a]	74[a]	154[a]	243[a]	457[a]	457[a]	319[a]	240[a]	334[a]
4	Glove Workers...............	....	....	....	....	....	....	30[a]	20[a]	11[a]	8[a]	8[a]
5	Hatters......................	*56*[a]	*58*[a]	*59*[a]	*76*[a]	*72*[a]	*86*[a]	*90*[a]	*89*[a]	*89*[a]	*90*[a]	*95*[a]
6	Ladies' Garment Workers......	....	....	....	....	20[a]	21[a]	30[a]	22[a]	18[a]	13[a]	23[a]
7	Special Order, Clothing Makers.	....	....	....	*26*	*38*	*110*[a]	[b]	....	....	....	....
8	Straw and Ladies' Hatters......	....	....	....	....	....	....	....	....	....	....	....
9	Tailors.......................	50[a]	50[a]	50[a]	73[a]	93[a]	109[a]	138[a]	159[a]	160[a]	166[a]	167[a]
	Total in Group.............	146	151	151	249	377	589	770	776	623	538	650
	Food, Liquor and Tobacco											
1	Bakery Workers..............	20[a]	21[a]	31[a]	45[a]	64[a]	102[a]	154[a]	162[a]	120[a]	106[a]	110[a]
2	Brewery Workmen............	100[a]	100[a]	107[a]	183[a]	235[a]	291[a]	300[a]	305[a]	340[a]	360[a]	400[c]
3	Cigarmakers..................	*283*[a]	*287*[a]	*315*[a]	*371*[a]	*377*[a]	*412*[a]	*443*[a]	*468*[a]	*456*[a]	*454*[a]	*480*[a]
4	Flour Mill Employees..........	....	....	....	....	....	....	21[a]	21[a]	9[a]	7[a]	7[a]
5	Food Workers, Amal...........	....	....	....	....	....	....	....	....	....	....	....
6	Stogie Makers................	....	....	....	....	....	....	....	....	....	....	....
7	Tobacco Workers.............	41[a]	46[a]	41[a]	60[a]	43[a]	41[a]	52[a]	56[a]	54[a]	55[a]	51[a]
	Total in Group.............	444	454	494	659	719	846	970	1012	979	982	1048
	Lumber and Woodworking											
1	Box Makers and Sawyers.......	....	....	....	....	....	....	....	....	....	....	....
2	Coopers......................	*15*[a]	*24*[a]	*32*[a]	*43*[a]	*57*[a]	*64*[a]	*79*[a]	*69*[a]	*58*[a]	*58*[a]	*57*[a]
3	Piano and Organ Workers......	....	*33*	*47*	*61*	*77*	57[a]	65[a]	99[a]	90[a]	80[a]	50[a]
4	Timber Workers[m]............	....	....	....	....	....	....	13[a]	14[a]	16[a]	17[a]	18[a]
5	Upholsterers..................	....	....	....	13[a]	13[a]	13[a]	25[a]	30[a]	28[a]	26[a]	26[a]
6	Wood Carvers................	*7*	9[a]	12[a]	18[a]	20[a]	23[a]	24[a]	21[a]	16[a]	16[a]	16[a]
7	Woodsmen and Saw Mill Workers	....	....	....	....	....	....	....	....	11[a]	12[a]	10[a]
8	Wood Workers................	33[a]	51[a]	68[a]	121[a]	151[a]	184[a]	273[a]	283[a]	200[a]	150[a]	93[a]
	Total in Group.............	55	117	159	256	318	341	479	516	419	359	270
	Restaurant and Trade											
1	Agents' Assn..................	11[a]	7[a]	9[a]	[b]	....	....	....	....	....	....	....
2	Butcher Workmen.............	....	....	....	....	....	....	....	....	....	....	....
3	Hotel Employees..............	15[a]	25[a]	20[a]	48[a]	103[a]	191[a]	391[a]	494[a]	387[a]	345[a]	363[a]
4	Hotel Workers................	....	....	....	....	....	....	....	....	....	....	....
5	Meat Cutters.................	11[a]	10[a]	17[a]	32[a]	55[a]	84[a]	253[a]	344[a]	62[a]	50[a]	53[a]
6	Retail Clerks.................	27[a]	50[a]	75[a]	200[a]	250[a]	300[a]	500[a]	500[a]	500[a]	500[a]	500[a]
	Total in Group.............	64	92	121	280	408	575	1144	1338	949	895	916

Trade Unions, 1897–1923 — *Continued*

1908	1909	1910	1911	1912	1913	1914	1915	1916	1917	1918	1919	1920	1921	1922	1923	
320[a]	320[a]	325[a]	327[a]	333[a]	343[a]	381[a]	356[a]	390[a]	396[a]	358[a]	368[a]	467[a]	410[a]	402[a]	399[a]	1
....	....	*22*	*15*	*15*	*7*	*7*	....	....	....	....	....	....	....	....	....	2
....	....	....	....	....	....	....	....	....	....	*20*	*30*	*35*	*42*	*46*	*52*	3
40[a]	40[a]	37[a]	26[a]	20[a]	19[a]	18[a]	18[a]	18[a]	[b]	....	....	....	....	....	....	4
8[a]	8[a]	8[a]	6[a]	6[a]	[e]	....	....	....	....	....	....	....	....	....	....	5
....	....	....	....	....	....	....	....	....	32[a]	41[a]	67[a]	117[a]	80[a]	34[a]	20[a]	6
25	*25*	*25*	*25*	*25*	*25*	*25*	*25*	*40*	*100*	*100*	*180*	*180*	*180*	*200*	*260*	7
....	....	45[d]	89[d]	152[d]	*144*	*140*[d]	*120*	*150*	*200*	*230*	*390*	*330*	*250*	*220*	[b]	8
5[a]	5[a]	6[a]	8[a]	9[a]	9[a]	9[a]	9[a]	10[a]	[b]	....	....	....	....	....	....	9
398	398	468	496	560	547	580	528	608	728	749	1035	1129	962	902	731	
13[a]	15[a]	21[a]	22[a]	28[a]	38[a]	36[a]	30[a]	63[a]	88[a]	*94*	*95*	*106*	*100*	*100*	*120*	1
....	....	....	....	....	....	....	*380*	*480*	*570*	*810*	*1440*	*1770*	*1430*	*1300*	*1340*	2
439[a]	534[a]	542[a]	525[a]	464[a]	585[a]	607[a]	422[a]	430[a]	449[a]	459[a]	460[a]	459[a]	472[a]	475[a]	476[a]	3
8[a]	8[a]	8[a]	9[a]	11[a]	13[a]	11[a]	10[a]	10[a]	8[a]	7[a]	7[a]	10[a]	7[a]	4[a]	2[a]	4
92[a]	*96*[a]	*97*[a]	*104*[a]	*94*[a]	*89*[a]	*90*[a]	85[a]	85[a]	85[a]	91[a]	100[a]	105[a]	115[a]	115[a]	115[a]	5
16[a]	18[a]	187[a]	668[a]	584[a]	788[a]	699[a]	653[a]	851[a]	823[a]	895[a]	905[a]	1054[a]	941[a]	939[a]	912[a]	6
....	....	....	....	....	....	....	....	....	....	....	....	....	....	....	....	7
....	....	*4*	*5*	*5*	*6*	*7*	....	....	....	....	....	....	....	....	....	8
161[a]	132[a]	117[a]	120[a]	120[a]	120[a]	120[a]	120[a]	120[a]	120[a]	120[a]	120[a]	120[a]	120[a]	120[a]	119[a]	9
729	803	976	1453	1306	1639	1570	1700	2039	2143	2476	3127	3624	3185	3053	3084	
105[a]	107[a]	127[a]	138[a]	146[a]	151[a]	157[a]	158[a]	175[a]	189[a]	204[a]	210[a]	275[a]	280[a]	248[a]	229[a]	1
425[a]	*452*[a]	*454*[a]	533[a c]	*625*[a]	650[a c]	*676*[a]	520[a]	496[a]	450[a]	450[a]	400[a]	341[a]	273[a]	190[a]	166[a]	2
471[a]	*515*[a]	*514*[a]	*500*[a]	*485*[a]	*485*[a]	*485*[a]	394[a]	377[a]	416[a]	395[a]	363[a]	388[a]	342[a]	320[a]	309[a]	3
8[a]	8[a]	3[a]	3[d]	[b]	....	....	....	....	....	....	....	....	....	....	....	4
....	....	....	....	....	....	....	....	....	....	....	....	....	*120*	*140*	*140*	5
....	....	*15*	*15*	*15*	15[d]	*14*	....	....	....	....	....	....	....	....	....	6
46[a]	43[a]	41[a]	40[a]	37[a]	36[a]	37[a]	39[a]	34[a]	32[a]	33[a]	42[a]	152[a]	123[a]	34[a]	19[a]	7
1055	1125	1154	1229	1308	1337	1369	1111	1082	1087	1082	1015	1156	1138	932	863	
....	....	*100*	*110*	137[d]	*122*	*123*	*110*	*80*	*70*	[b]	....	....	....	....	....	1
47[a]	*43*[a]	*44*[a]	*48*[a]	*45*[a]	*47*[a]	*44*[a]	39[a]	36[a]	39[a]	40[a]	40[a]	43[a]	44[a]	28[a]	17[a]	2
50[a]	40[a]	40[a]	40[a]	20[a]	10[a]	10[a]	10[a]	10[a]	15[a]	20[a]	20[a]	32[a]	27[a]	9[a]	7[a]	3
17[a]	18[a]	18[a]	15[a]	15[a]	31[a]	25[a]	7[a]	4[a]	7[a]	23[a]	32[a]	101[a]	58[a]	8[a]	[b]	4
28[a]	28[a]	28[a]	28[a]	28[a]	31[a]	35[a]	35[a]	39[a]	40[a]	48[a]	55[a]	56[a]	60[a]	67[a]	73[a]	5
13[a]	13[a]	12[a]	12[a]	10[a]	10[a]	11[a]	10[a]	11[a]	12[a]	12[a]	10[a]	12[a]	12[a]	11[a]	9[a]	6
3[a]	7[a]	6[a]	6[d]	[b]	....	....	....	....	....	....	....	....	....	....	....	7
40[a]	41[a]	32[a]	31[a]	[b]	....	....	....	....	....	....	....	....	....	....	....	8
198	190	280	290	255	251	248	211	180	183	143	157	244	201	123	106	
....	....	....	....	....	....	....	....	....	....	....	....	....	....	....	....	1
....	....	*20*	*20*	*20*	*23*	20[d]	*18*	*17*	*15*	[b]	....	....	....	....	....	2
386[a]	368[a]	370[a]	430[a]	476[a]	539[a]	590[a]	606[a]	590[a]	646[a]	652[a]	608[a]	604[a]	572[a]	465[a]	384[a]	3
....	....	....	....	....	147[d]	126[d]	....	....	....	....	....	....	....	....	....	4
63[a]	63[a]	54[a]	31[a]	40[a]	54[a]	62[a]	61[a]	73[a]	96[a]	291[a]	663[a]	653[a]	439[a]	196[a]	104[a]	5
500[a]	150[a]	150[a]	150[a]	150[a]	150[a]	150[a]	150[a]	150[a]	150[a]	150[a]	150[a]	208[a]	212[a]	167[a]	103[a]	6
949	581	594	631	686	913	948	835	830	907	1093	1421	1465	1223	828	591	

Table I. — Membership of American

	Name of Union	1897	1898	1899	1900	1901	1902	1903	1904	1905	1906	1907
	Transportation											
1	Commercial Telegraphers	....	....	....	....	....	....	10[a]	20[a]	20[a]	20[a]	35[a]
2	Locomotive Engineers	*303*	*307*	*317*	*356*	*380*	*415*	*464*	*500*	*536*	*569*	*622*
3	Locomotive Firemen	*243*	*270*	*307*	*360*	*390*	*433*	*435*	*544*	*550*	*570*	*617*
4	Longshoremen	50[a]	80[a]	130[a]	200[a]	250[a]	347[a]	400[a]	500[a]	478[a]	340[a]	320[a]
5	Maintenance of Way Employees	....	....	....	*30*	38[c]	46[a]	87[a]	123[a]	120[a]	120[a]	132[a]
6	Marine Engineers	*39*	*40*	*49*	*60*	*69*	*78*	*87*	*97*	*95*	*96*	*101*
7	Masters, Mates and Pilots	....	....	....	....	....	....	....	....	....	....	....
8	Mechanical Trackmen	....	....	....	....	....	....	....	....	....	....	....
9	Pavers	....	....	....	....	....	....	....	....	10[a]	12[a]	15[a]
10	Paving Cutters	....	....	....	....	1[a]	2[a]	9[a]	12[a]	13[a]	15[a]	18[a]
11	Pilots' Ass'n, Lake	....	....	....	....	....	....	....	....	....	10[a]	[b]
12	Railroad Freight Handlers	....	....	....	....	....	....	48[a]	33[a]	34[a]	32[a]	63[a]
13	Railroad Patrolmen	....	....	....	....	....	....	....	....	....	....	....
14	Railroad Signalmen	....	....	....	....	....	....	....	....	....	....	....
15	Railroad Station Agents	....	....	....	....	....	....	....	....	....	....	....
16	Railroad Stationmen	....	....	....	....	....	....	....	....	....	....	....
17	Railroad Station Employees	....	....	....	....	....	....	....	....	....	....	....
18	Railroad Telegraphers	....	....	80[a]	80[a]	80[a]	80[a]	95[a]	150[a]	150[a]	150[a]	150[a]
19	Railroad Trainmen	*254*	*312*	*372*	*432*	*468*	*550*	*682*	*745*	*785*	*869*	*1000*
20	Railway Clerks	....	....	....	5[a]	6[a]	*13*	*21*	*29*	*37*	*51*	*88*
21	Railway Clerks, Ass'n	....	....	....	....	....	....	13[a]	6[a]	[b]	....	....
22	Railway Conductors	*207*	*219*	*233*	*246*	*259*	*279*	*313*	*334*	*357*	*384*	*414*
23	Railway Express Messengers	....	....	....	....	....	....	....	....	....	....	....
24	Railway Expressmen	....	....	....	....	....	....	14[a]	3[a]	[b]	....	....
25	Railway Employees of N. A.	....	....	....	....	....	....	....	....	....	....	....
26	Seamen	40[a]	40[a]	40[a]	42[a]	82[a]	99[a]	139[a]	201[a]	195[a]	194[a]	248[a]
27	Steam Shovelmen	....	....	....	....	....	....	....	....	....	....	....
28	Sleeping Car Conductors	....	....	....	....	....	....	....	....	....	....	....
29	Street and Electric Railway Employees	28[a]	30[a]	30[a]	35[a]	43[a]	98[a]	256[a]	300[a]	300[a]	300[a]	320[a]
30	Switchmen	....	....	....	....	....	....	....	....	....	81[a]	92[a]
31	Teamsters	....	....	17[a]	47[a]	94[a]	138[a]	320[a]	840[a]	783[a]	402[a]	366[a]
32	Tunnel Constructors	....	....	....	....	....	....	....	....	....	....	....
	Total in Group	1164	1298	1575	1893	2160	2578	3393	4437	4463	4215	4601
	Paper, Printing and Bookbinding											
1	Bookbinders	*26*	26[a]	28[a]	36[a]	53[a]	70[a]	81[a]	65[a]	66[a]	68[a]	89[a]
2	Lithographers	*15*	*16*[h]	*17*[h]	*18*[h]	*20*	*23*[c]	*27*[c]	*30*	*30*	30[a]	23[a]
3	Lithographic Press Feeders	....	....	....	....	....	....	....	....	....	....	....
4	Lithographic Workmen	....	....	....	....	....	....	....	....	....	....	....
5	Machine Printers	....	....	....	....	....	....	4[a]	4[a]	4[a]	5[a]	5[a]
6	Paper Makers	1[a]	1[a]	1[a]	4[a]	18[a]	41[a]	107[a]	88[a]	50[a]	35[a]	31[a]
7	Paper Box Workers	....	....	....	....	....	....	....	12[a]	9[a]	7[a]	[b]
8	Photo Engravers	....	....	....	*4*	*6*	*8*	*8*	17[a]	22[a]	22[a]	28[a]
9	Poster Artists	....	....	....	....	....	....	....	....	....	....	....
10	Print Cutters	....	....	....	....	....	....	3[a]	3[a]	4[a]	4[a]	4[a]
11	Printing Pressmen	50[a]	58[a]	72[a]	91[a]	100[a]	119[a]	144[a]	160[a]	170[a]	166[a]	166[a]
12	Pulp and Paper Mill Workers	....	....	....	....	....	*25*	*45*	*45*	*45*	*45*	*45*
13	Steel Plate Engravers	....	....	....	....	....	....	....	....	....	....	....
14	Steel Plate Printers	*6*	4[a]	4[a]	6[a]	7[a]	7[a]	9[a]	10[a]	11[a]	12[a]	12[a]
15	Steel Plate Transferers	....	....	....	....	....	....	....	....	....	1[a]	1[a]
16	Stereotypers and Electrotypers	....	....	....	....	....	18[a]	21[a]	24[a]	28[a]	28[a]	29[a]
17	Tip Printers	....	....	....	....	....	....	2[a]	2[a]	2[a]	2[a]	1[a]
18	Typographical Union	*281*[a]	*286*[a]	*306*[a]	*321*[a]	*349*[a]	*386*[a]	*424*[a]	*462*[a]	*467*[a]	*450*[a]	*423*[a]
19	Wall Paper Crafts	....	....	....	....	....	....	....	....	....	....	....
	Total in Group	379	391	428	480	553	697	875	922	908	875	857

1908	1909	1910	1911	1912	1913	1914	1915	1916	1917	1918	1919	1920	1921	1922	1923	
19[a]	10[a]	10[a]	10[a]	10[a]	10[a]	10[a]	10[a]	10[a]	10[a]	10[a]	20[a]	22[a]	32[a]	34[a]	26[a]	1
629	*637*	*674*	*699*	*719*	*739*	*738*	*737*	*729*	*752*	*808*	*831*	*869*	*878*	*861*	*874*	2
665	*652*	*692*	*768*	*853*	*911*	*868*	*831*	*936*	*1030*	*1134*	*1233*	*1259*	*1122*	*1073*	*1180*	3
315[a]	213[a]	208[a]	250[a]	235[a]	220[a]	250[a]	250[a]	250[a]	255[a]	260[a]	313[a]	740[a]	641[a]	463[a]	343[a]	4
135[a]	100[a]	87[a]	100[a]	91[a]	80[a]	65[a]	81[a]	89[a]	97[a]	56[a]	542[a]	501[cj]	460[cj]	419[cj]	377[a]	5
109	*109*	*100*	*100*	*95*	*92*	*91*	*91*	*93*	*105*	79[a]	128[a]	170[a]	211[a]	190[a]	*111*	6
....	....	*60*	*60*	*60*[c]	60[d]	50[d]	*45*	40[a]	43[a]	48[a]	62[a]	71[a]	91[a]	55[a]	41[a]	7
....	....	....	....	....	*3*	*3*	....	....	....	....	....	....	....	....	....	8
15[a]	15[a]	15[a]	15[a]	15[a]	15[a]	16[a]	16[a]	15[a]	15[a]	17[a]	18[a]	19[a]	20[a]	20[a]	20[a]	9
20[a]	26[a]	32[a]	32[a]	35[a]	35[a]	35[a]	35[a]	33[a]	32[a]	32[a]	26[a]	26[a]	24[a]	24[a]	24[a]	10
....	....	....	....	....	....	....	....	....	....	....	....	....	....	....	....	11
78[a]	46[a]	47[a]	40[a]	25[a]	10[a]	29[a]	•	....	....	....	....	....	....	....	....	12
....	....	....	....	....	....	....	....	....	....	....	....	26[a]	16[a]	9[a]	•	13
....	....	*12*	*8*	10[d]	8[d]	7[ad]	8[a]	9[a]	8[a]	9[a]	62[a]	123[a]	113[a]	105[a]	89[a]	14
....	....	*6*	*5*	*5*	*5*	11[d]	*35*	*35*	*40*	*45*	*50*	*88*	....	....	....	15
....	....	....	....	....	....	....	....	....	....	*61*	*45*	*33*	21[k]	....	....	16
....	....	*22*	*26*	28[d]	35[d]	43[d]	*134*	*187*	*222*	*294*	*327*	*352*	*300*	*270*	*210*	17
150[a]	150[a]	200[a]	250[a]	250[a]	250[a]	250[a]	250[a]	250[a]	272[a]	377[a]	446[a]	*780*[a]	*720*[a]	*670*[a]	*680*[a]	18
1007	*1027*	*1139*	*1191*	*1243*	*1338*	*1261*	*1305*	*1432*	*1591*	*1814*	*1969*	*1846*	*1772*	*1698*	*1789*	19
91	56[a]	50[a]	50[a]	50[a]	50[a]	50[a]	50[a]	51[a]	68[a]	172[a]	714[a]	1860[a]	1696[a]	1378[a]	961[a]	20
....	....	....	....	....	....	....	....	....	....	....	....	....	....	....	....	21
424	*438*	*460*	*474*	*479*	*492*	*491*	*485*	*481*	*487*	*503*	*524*	*560*	*580*	*620*	*600*	22
....	....	....	....	2[a]	1[a]	[b]	....	....	....	....	....	....	....	....	....	23
....	....	....	....	....	....	....	....	....	....	....	....	....	....	....	....	24
....	....	....	....	....	....	....	....	....	....	....	....	200[k]	360[k]	....	....	25
255[a]	168[a]	160[a]	160[a]	160[a]	160[a]	160[a]	160[a]	217[a]	322[a]	371[a]	427[a]	659[a]	1033[a]	492[a]	179[a]	26
....	....	*13*	*14*	*16*	*18*	*18*	27[a]	20[a]	29[a]	37[a]	*60*	*80*	*96*	*101*	*112*	27
....	....	....	....	....	....	....	....	....	....	....	....	12[a]	25[a]	26[a]	23[a]	28
320[a]	333[a]	367[a]	393[a]	402[a]	457[a]	545[a]	589[a]	646[a]	737[a]	786[a]	897[a]	987[a]	1000[a]	1000[a]	1000[a]	29
93[a]	80[a]	80[a]	87[a]	87[a]	96[a]	98[a]	90[a]	93[a]	102[a]	107[a]	118[a]	140[a]	101[a]	88[a]	87[a]	30
377[a]	320[a]	358[a]	382[a]	415[a]	469[a]	511[a]	516[a]	590[a]	703[a]	729[a]	756[a]	1108[a]	1057[a]	764[a]	727[a]	31
....	....	13[a]	17[a]	18[a]	19[a]	17[a]	15[a]	27[a]	34[a]	24[a]	20[a]	30[a]	30[a]	30[a]	30[a]	32
4702	4380	4805	5131	5303	5573	5617	5760	6233	6954	7773	9588	12561	12399	10390	9483	
79[a]	71[a]	78[a]	79[a]	85[a]	91[a]	94[a]	85[a]	93[a]	114[a]	145[a]	164[a]	207[a]	247[a]	163[a]	129[a]	1
11[a]	13[a]	17[a]	21[a]	24[a]	26[a]	28[a]	35[a]	42[a]	46[a]	49[a]	56[a]	61[a]	72[a]	76[a]	63[a]	2
....	10[a]	9[a]	9[a]	9[a]	10[a]	*10*	*4*	*4*	*4*	*4*	[b]	....	....	....	....	3
....	....	*3*	*3*	*4*	*5*	*5*	....	....	....	....	....	....	....	....	....	4
5[a]	5[a]	5[a]	5[a]	5[a]	5[a]	5[a]	5[a]	5[a]	5[a]	5[a]	5[a]	5[a]	5[a]	5[a]	[l]	5
43[a]	10[a]	16[a]	24[a]	28[a]	40[a]	44[a]	45[a]	52[a]	64[a]	60[a]	57[a]	74[a]	107[a]	83[a]	70[a]	6
....	....	....	....	....	....	....	....	....	....	....	....	....	....	....	....	7
29[a]	32[a]	35[a]	37[a]	40[a]	44[a]	47[a]	48[a]	51[a]	51[a]	51[a]	50[a]	59[a]	65[a]	65[a]	65[a]	8
....	....	*3*	*3*	*3*	*3*	*4*	*4*	*4*	*4*	*4*	*4*	*4*	*4*[h]	*4*[h]	*4*[h]	9
4[a]	4[a]	4[a]	4[a]	4[a]	4[a]	4[a]	4[a]	4[a]	4[a]	4[a]	4[a]	4[a]	4[a]	3[a]	[l]	10
172[a]	178[a]	186[a]	190[a]	190[a]	190[a]	193[a]	227[a]	290[a]	330[a]	340[a]	340[a]	350[a]	370[a]	370[a]	370[a]	11
45	10[a]	7[a]	28[a]	35[a]	31[a]	35[a]	43[a]	44[a]	65[a]	80[a]	84[a]	95[a]	113[a]	68[a]	46[a]	12
....	....	....	....	....	....	....	....	....	....	....	1[a]	2[a]	4[a]	3[a]	2[a]	13
12[a]	12[a]	13[a]	13[a]	12[a]	13[a]	13[a]	13[a]	12[a]	13[a]	12[a]	13[a]	14[a]	15[a]	15[a]	12[a]	14
1[a]	1[a]	1[a]	1[a]	1[a]	1[a]	1[a]	1[a]	1[a]	1[a]	1[a]	1[a]	1[a]	1[a]	1[a]	[b]	15
31[a]	35[a]	40[a]	42[a]	43[a]	45[a]	45[a]	49[a]	49[a]	52[a]	53[a]	54[a]	59[a]	61[a]	60[a]	62[a]	16
2[a]	2[a]	2[a]	2[a]	2[a]	2[a]	•	*2*	3[a]	3[a]	3[a]	[b]	....	....	....	....	17
437[a]	*449*[a]	*478*[a]	*511*[a]	*538*[a]	*556*[a]	*585*[a]	591[a]	607[a]	616[a]	633[a]	647[a]	705[a]	748[a]	689[a]	681[a]	18
....	....	....	....	....	....	....	....	....	....	....	....	....	....	....	7[a]	19
871	832	897	972	1023	1066	1113	1156	1261	1372	1444	1480	1640	1816	1605	1511	

TABLE I. — MEMBERSHIP OF AMERICAN

	Name of Union	1897	1898	1899	1900	1901	1902	1903	1904	1905	1906	1907
	Theatres and Music											
1	Actors and Artists	....	....	....	....	....	....	....	....	....	....	....
2	Actors' Protective Union	....	....	....	....	3[a]	5[a]	11[a]	11[a]	11[a]	11[a]	11[a]
3	Musical and Theatrical Union	....	....	....	....	....	....	....	....	....	....	....
4	Musicians	46[a]	60[a]	60[a]	62[a]	81[a]	97[a]	140[a]	220[a]	308[a]	354[a]	375[a]
5	Theatrical Stage Employees	20[a]	23[a]	30[a]	30[a]	38[a]	44[a]	45[a]	50[a]	55[a]	60[a]	60[a]
6	White Rats Actors' Union	....	....	....	....	*5*	*1*	*1*	*1*	*1*	*1*	*6*
	Total in Group	66	83	90	92	127	147	197	282	375	426	452
	Chemical, Clay, Glass and Stone											
1	Brick and Tile Workers	8[a]	5[a]	10[a]	14[a]	17[a]	41[a]	55[a]	73[a]	41[a]	64[a]	43[a]
2	Flint Glass Workers	*72*[a]	*71*[a]	*71*[a]	*80*[a]	*91*[a]	*69*[a]	*69*	*69*	*69*	*69*	*69*
3	Glass Bottle Blowers	*40*	*40*	42[a]	42[a]	47[a]	59[a]	61[a]	66[a]	70[a]	78[a]	80[a]
4	Glass Flatteners	....	5[a]	6[a]	6[a]	....	[e]	....	....	....	....	....
5	Glass House Employees	....	....	....	....	....	....	6[a]	6[a]	2[a]	2[a]	[b]
6	Glass Workers, Amal.	....	....	....	2[a]	3[a]	7[a]	20[a]	17[a]	17[a]	16[a]	14[a]
7	Granite Cutters	45[a]	46[a]	48[a]	59[a]	70[a]	82[a]	94[a]	99[a]	103[a]	113[a]	126[a]
8	Potters, Operative	*5*	*8*	13[a]	22[a]	29[a]	49[a]	61[a]	58[a]	56[a]	56[a]	58[a]
9	Potters	2[a]	2[a]	....	....	....	[b]	....	....	....	....	....
10	Powder Workers	....	....	....	....	....	4[a]	7[a]	7[a]	5[a]	6[a]	5[a]
11	Stone Cutters	*60*	*65*	*70*	*75*	*75*	*80*	*80*	*80*	*80*	*80*	85[a]
12	Stoneware Potters	1[a]	1[a]	1[a]	1[a]	....	....	[b]	....	....	....	....
13	Window Glass Cutters	....	8[a]	8[a]	....	....	[e]	....	....	....	....	....
14	Window Glass Snappers	....	....	....	....	....	....	9[a]	11[a]	12[a]	10[a]	6[a]
15	Window Glass Workers	....	....	....	....	....	....	....	....	*58*	*57*[a]	*66*[a]
	Total in Group	233	251	269	301	332	391	462	486	513	551	552
	Miscellaneous											
1	Barbers	22[a]	30[a]	40[a]	69[a]	116[a]	160[a]	208[a]	236[a]	227[a]	231[a]	241[a]
2	Bill Posters	....	....	....	....	....	....	10[a]	13[a]	14[a]	14[a]	14[a]
3	Broommakers	1[e]	1[a]	3[a]	4[a]	8[a]	9[a]	11[a]	11[a]	10[a]	10[a]	9[a]
4	Brushmakers	....	....	....	....	....	....	....	7[a]	7[a]	5[a]	5[a]
5	Fur Work, Assn.	....	....	....	....	....	....	....	3[a]	4[a]	4[a]	4[a]
6	Fur Workers	....	....	....	....	....	....	....	....	....	....	....
7	Horse Shoers	20[a]	20[a]	20[a]	21[a]	23[a]	28[a]	44[a]	42[a]	42[a]	41[a]	44[a]
8	I. W. W. (Chicago)	....	....	....	....	....	....	....	....	*143*	*104*	*67*
9	I. W. W. (Detroit)	....	....	....	....	....	....	....	....	....	....	....
10	Laundry Workers	....	....	....	....	21[a]	42[a]	80[a]	65[a]	46[a]	55[a]	31[a]
11	Lobster Fishermen	....	....	....	....	....	....	....	....	....	....	.. 6[a]
12	Mattress Workers	....	....	....	....	....	....	....	15[a]	15[a]	[b]	....
13	Oil and Gas Well Workers	....	....	....	4[a]	5[a]	3[a]	4[a]	4[a]	4[a]	[b]	....
14	Rubber Workers	....	....	....	....	....	....	10[a]	2[a]	1[a]	[e]	....
15	Stationary Firemen	....	....	11[a]	24[a]	41[a]	62[a]	143[a]	180[a]	122[a]	123[a]	125[a]
16	Steam Engineers	7[a]	12[a]	18[a]	27[a]	48[a]	65[a]	142[a]	176[a]	175[a]	175[a]	175[a]
17	Trade and Federal Unions (A. F. of L.)	142[a]	146[a]	163[a]	349[a]	469[a]	678[a]	828[a]	553[a]	1046[a]	759[a]	713[a]
	Total in Group	192	209	255	498	731	1047	1480	1307	1856	1521	1434
	Total in All Groups	4470	5007	6110	8685	11247	13759	19139	20727	20223	19587	21228

NOTES TO TABLE I

[a] Affiliated with the American Federation of Labor.

[b] Union disbanded or amalgamated with another union or withdrawn.

[c] Average of preceding and following year.

[d] From the New York Labor Bulletin.

[e] Union suspended or not recognized by American Federation of Labor, or charter surrenderd or revoked

[f] No figures published. The number reported by the Canadian Department of Labour seems to be inaccurate.

[g] The union now reports for 1911–1912, 7,000 members.

[h] Estimated.

[i] Refused to give figures for later years.

[j] This union does not deem it a wise policy to

TRADE UNIONS, 1897–1923 — *Continued*

1908	1909	1910	1911	1912	1913	1914	1915	1916	1917	1918	1919	1920	1921	1922	1923	
....	....	....	....	....	....	....	87[a]	90[a]	*30*[an]	*37*[an]	*40*[an]	*90*[an]	*120*[an]	*127*[an]	*130*[an]	1
11[a]	11[a]	11[a]	[b]	....	....	....	....	....	....	....	....	....	....	....	....	2
....	....	*20*	*30*	50[d]	35[d]	60[d]	....	....	....	....	....	....	....	....	....	3
375[a]	394[a]	400[a]	500[a]	500[a]	546[a]	600[a]	600[a]	600[a]	604[a]	650[a]	654[a]	700[a]	746[a]	750[a]	750[a]	4
62[a]	80[a]	91[a]	98[a]	110[a]	132[a]	150[a]	180[a]	181[a]	186[a]	186[a]	185[a]	196[a]	194[a]	195[a]	196[a]	5
20	*40*	*80*	66[a]	110[a]	110[a]	110[a]	....	....	....	....	....	....	....	....	....	6
468	525	602	694	770	823	920	867	871	820	873	879	986	1060	1072	1076	
28[a]	25[a]	38[a]	34[a]	34[a]	39[a]	32[a]	29[a]	32[a]	28[a]	25[a]	27[a]	52[a]	54[a]	41[a]	48[a]	1
70	*81*	*89*	89[d]	87[d]	91[a]	99[a]	94[a]	94[a]	98[a]	99[a]	95[a]	99[a]	97[a]	87[a]	81[a]	2
88[a]	93[a]	100[a]	100[a]	100[a]	100[a]	100[a]	100[a]	100[a]	100[a]	100[a]	100[a]	100[a]	100[a]	97[a]	70[a]	3
....	....	....	....	....	....	....	....	....	....	....	....	....	....	....	....	4
....	....	....	....	....	....	....	....	....	....	....	....	....	....	....	....	5
12[a]	11[a]	12[a]	12[a]	11[a]	13[a]	12[a]	11[a]	[b]	....	....	....	....	....	....	....	6
130[a]	131[a]	134[a]	135[a]	135[a]	135[a]	135[a]	135[a]	131[a]	125[a]	119[a]	107[a]	105[a]	105[a]	100[a]	95[a]	7
59[a]	59[a]	58[a]	59[a]	65[a]	65[a]	77[a]	78[a]	77[a]	76[a]	78[a]	74[a]	80[a]	91[a]	92[a]	91[a]	8
....	....	....	....	....	....	....	....	....	....	....	....	....	....	....	....	9
5[a]	2[a]	2[a]	2[a]	2[a]	2[a]	2[a]	2[a]	3[a]	3[a]	4[a]	3[a]	3[a]	2[a]	2[a]	3[a]	10
83[a]	89[a]	80[a]	86[a]	89[a]	66[a]	60[a]	44[a]	43[a]	41[a]	42[a]	39[a]	40[a]	44[a]	46[a]	49[a]	11
....	....	....	....	....	....	....	....	....	....	....	....	....	....	....	....	12
....	....	....	....	....	....	....	....	....	....	....	....	....	....	....	....	13
10	*14*	18[d]	15[e]	12[d]	12[d]	22[d]	....	....	....	....	....	....	....	....	....	14
67[h]	69[h]	70[d]	62[d]	60[d]	40[d]	39[d]	*38*	*41*	*46*	*43*[a]	*37*[a]	*38*[a]	*38*[a]	*32*[a]	*16*[a]	15
552	574	601	594	595	563	578	531	521	517	510	482	517	531	497	453	
255[a]	255[a]	265[a]	285[a]	299[a]	318[a]	343[a]	341[a]	359[a]	398[a]	384[a]	359[a]	442[a]	470[a]	452[a]	432[a]	1
14[a]	14[a]	14[a]	14[a]	14[a]	14[a]	14[a]	14[a]	15[a]	15[a]	16[a]	16[a]	16[a]	16[a]	16[a]	16[a]	2
8[a]	8[a]	6[a]	7[a]	7[a]	7[a]	7[a]	7[a]	8[a]	7[a]	7[a]	10[a]	14[a]	12[a]	8[a]	7[a]	3
4[a]	2[a]	2[a]	2[a]	2[a]	2[a]	2[a]	2[a]	2[a]	2[a]	2[a]	[b]	....	....	....	....	4
4[a]	2[a]	2[a]	[e]	....	....	....	....	....	....	....	....	....	....	....	....	5
....	....	....	....	....	....	8[a]	37[a]	57[a]	81[a]	100[a]	108[a]	121[a]	45[a]	47[a]	92[a]	6
61[a]	72[a]	72[a]	49[a]	52[a]	53[a]	57[a]	57[a]	58[a]	54[a]	54[a]	54[a]	54[a]	54[a]	25[a]	20[a]	7
132	*107*	*91*	*128*	*183*	*143*	*120*	[o]	....	....	....	....	....	....	....	....	8
....	....	....	*35*	*107*	*50*	*20*	[o]	....	....	....	....	....	....	....	....	9
40[a]	35[a]	29[a]	26[a]	26[a]	26[a]	28[a]	41[a]	43[a]	46[a]	55[a]	60[a]	67[a]	70[a]	65[a]	55[a]	10
6[a]	[b]	....	....	....	....	....	....	....	....	....	....	....	....	....	....	11
....	....	....	....	....	....	....	....	....	....	....	....	....	....	....	....	12
....	....	....	....	....	....	....	....	....	....	....	45[a]	209[a]	248[a]	61[a]	25[a]	13
....	....	....	....	....	....	....	....	....	....	....	....	....	....	....	....	14
173[a]	107[a]	81[a]	80[a]	114[a]	160[a]	160[a]	160[a]	170[a]	170[a]	171[a]	205[a]	296[a]	350[a]	250[a]	125[a]	15
168[a]	161[a]	160[a]	160[a]	177[a]	200[a]	203[a]	210[a]	210[a]	220[a]	230[a]	250[a]	320[a]	320[a]	320[a]	271[a]	16
616[a]	608[a]	647[a]	680[a]	590[a]	659[a]	570[a]	489[a]	705[a]	1016[a]	1076[a]	1091[a]	1498[a]	1027[a]	747[a]	581[a]	17
1481	1371	1369	1466	1571	1632	1532	1358	1627	2009	2095	2198	3037	2612	1991	1624	
21306	20474	21842	23828	24835	27534	27169	26077.	28080	31046	35084	41691	51108	48150	40594	37800	

NOTES TO TABLE I—*Continued*

publish its membership figures for these years. The membership has therefore been estimated by the process of simple interpolation on the assumption that the fall in membership in 1919 to 1923 was a gradual one. This assumption is probably contrary to the facts in that the fall from 1920 to 1921 was more precipitate But in the absence of the data no other assumption can be used.

[k] From the Canadian Department of Labour, *Report on Labour Organizations.*

[l] Amalgamated to form the United Wall Paper Crafts.

[m] Sometimes called Shingle Weavers.

[n] The source of these figures is the Actors' Equity Association.

[o] Figures not available for later years.

TABLE II. — MEMBERSHIP OF AFFILIATED AND

(00's

Group	1897	1898	1899	1900	1901	1902	1903	1904	1905	1906	1907
Mining and Quarrying											
Affiliated	129	340	629	1167	1994	1768	2512	2548	2699	2367	2678
Independent	80	100	120	140	177	196	283	241	263	286	442
Total	209	440	749	1307	2171	1964	2795	2789	2962	2653	3120
Building Trades											
Affiliated	405	436	661	1134	1478	1968	3096	3194	2998	3200	3524
Independent	268	302	307	397	438	666	596	722	729	693	808
Total	673	738	968	1531	1916	2634	3692	3916	3727	3893	4332
Metal, Machinery and Shipbuilding											
Affiliated	467	450	576	775	985	1252	1830	1927	1466	1599	1763
Independent	34	12	13	34	53	121	222	206	189	274	360
Total	501	462	589	809	1038	1373	2052	2133	1655	1873	2123
Textile											
Affiliated	56	55	49	65	60	139	185	141	134	135	145
Independent	25	30	20	15	10	8	7	7	7	8	12
Total	81	85	69	80	70	147	192	148	141	143	157
Clothing											
Affiliated	146	151	151	223	339	589	770	776	623	538	650
Independent	0	0	0	26	38	0	0	0	0	0	0
Total	146	151	151	249	377	589	770	776	623	538	650
Leather											
Affiliated	126	98	53	71	126	215	397	406	383	380	377
Independent	26	26	27	25	25	25	25	25	25	25	25
Total	152	124	80	96	151	240	422	431	408	405	402
Transportation											
Affiliated	118	150	297	409	556	810	1391	2188	2103	1676	1759
Independent	1046	1148	1278	1484	1604	1768	2002	2249	2360	2539	2842
Total	1164	1298	1575	1893	2160	2578	3393	4437	4463	4215	4601
Paper, Printing and Bookbinding											
Affiliated	332	375	411	458	527	641	795	847	833	830	812
Independent	47	16	17	22	26	56	80	75	75	45	45
Total	379	391	428	480	553	697	875	922	908	875	857

INDEPENDENT NATIONAL TRADE UNIONS, 1897–1923

omitted)

1908	1909	1910	1911	1912	1913	1914	1915	1916	1917	1918	1919	1920	1921	1922	1923
2592	2718	2378	3107	3429	4315	3802	3322	3376	3734	4332	4146	4177	4449	3805	4154
305	353	371	0	0	0	0	0	0	0	0	0	0	0	0	0
2897	3071	2749	3107	3429	4315	3802	3322	3376	3734	4332	4146	4177	4449	3805	4154
3658	3652	3908	3960	3911	4375	4497	4457	4711	5905	7006	8018	8879	8691	8263	8444
788	607	682	828	1180	1158	923	870	818	160	0	0	0	0	0	0
4446	4259	4590	4788	5091	5533	5420	5327	5529	6065	7006	8018	8879	8691	8263	8444
1722	1563	1909	2039	1921	2028	2101	2078	2467	2872	3702	5768	7984	7213	4987	3523
279	215	54	64	122	161	158	164	204	225	260	407	604	70	70	60
2001	1778	1963	2103	2043	2189	2259	2242	2671	3097	3962	6175	8588	7283	5057	3583
160	131	131	132	142	196	215	224	289	406	494	590	1050	830	301	301
12	13	79	81	84	95	84	0	0	0	0	8	441	52	68	74
172	144	210	213	226	291	299	224	289	406	494	598	1491	882	369	375
729	803	972	1448	1301	1633	1563	1320	1559	1573	1572	1592	1748	1655	1653	1624
0	0	4	5	5	6	7	380	480	570	904	1535	1876	1530	1400	1460
729	803	976	1453	1306	1639	1570	1700	2039	2143	2476	3127	3624	3185	3053	3084
373	373	376	367	368	371	408	383	418	428	399	435	584	490	436	419
25	25	92	129	192	176	172	145	190	300	350	600	545	472	466	312
398	398	468	496	560	547	580	528	608	728	749	1035	1129	962	902	731
1777	1517	1627	1786	1795	1872	2043	2097	2340	2727	3114	4549	6773	6810	5348	4607
2925	2863	3178	3345	3508	3701	3574	3663	3893	4227	4659	5039	5788	5589	5042	4876
4702	4380	4805	5131	5303	5573	5617	5760	6233	6954	7773	9588	12561	12399	10390	9483
826	832	891	966	1016	1058	1094	1146	1253	1364	1436	1476	1636	1812	1601	1507
45	0	6	6	7	8	19	10	8	8	8	4	4	4	4	4
871	832	897	972	1023	1066	1113	1156	1261	1372	1444	1480	1640	1816	1605	1511

Table II. — Membership of Affiliated and Independent

(00's

Group	1897	1898	1899	1900	1901	1902	1903	1904	1905	1906	1907
Lumber and Woodworking											
Affiliated	48	84	112	195	241	341	479	516	419	359	270
Independent	7	33	47	61	77	0	0	0	0	0	0
Total	55	117	159	256	318	341	479	516	419	359	270
Chemical, Clay, Glass and Stone											
Affiliated	128	138	199	226	257	311	313	337	306	402	483
Independent	105	113	70	75	75	80	149	149	207	149	69
Total	233	251	269	301	332	391	462	486	513	551	552
Food, Liquor and Tobacco											
Affiliated	444	454	494	659	719	846	970	1012	979	982	648
Independent	0	0	0	0	0	0	0	0	0	0	400
Total	444	454	494	659	719	846	970	1012	979	982	1048
Restaurant and Trade											
Affiliated	64	92	121	280	408	575	1144	1338	949	895	916
Independent	0	0	0	0	0	0	0	0	0	0	0
Total	64	92	121	280	408	575	1144	1338	949	895	916
Theatres and Music											
Affiliated	66	83	90	92	122	146	196	281	374	425	446
Independent	0	0	0	0	5	1	1	1	1	1	6
Total	66	83	90	92	127	147	197	282	375	426	452
Public Service											
Affiliated	0	0	0	0	0	0	0	0	0	0	9
Independent	111	112	113	154	176	190	216	234	245	258	305
Total	111	112	113	154	176	190	216	234	245	258	314
Miscellaneous											
Affiliated	192	209	255	498	731	1047	1480	1307	1713	1417	1367
Independent	0	0	0	0	0	0	0	0	143	104	67
Total	192	209	255	498	731	1047	1480	1307	1856	1521	1434
Total Affiliated	2721	3115	4098	6252	8543	10648	15558	16818	15979	15205	15847
Total Independent	1749	1892	2012	2433	2704	3111	3581	3909	4244	4382	5381
Grand Total	4470	5007	6110	8685	11247	13759	19139	20727	20223	19587	21228

NATIONAL TRADE UNIONS, 1897–1923 — *Continued*

omitted)

1908	1909	1910	1911	1912	1913	1914	1915	1916	1917	1918	1919	1920	1921	1922	1923
198	190	180	174	118	129	125	101	100	113	143	157	244	201	123	106
0	0	100	116	137	122	123	110	80	70	0	0	0	0	0	0
198	190	280	290	255	251	248	211	180	183	143	157	244	201	123	106
405	410	424	428	436	511	517	493	480	471	510	482	517	531	497	453
147	164	177	166	159	52	61	38	41	46	0	0	0	0	0	0
552	574	601	594	595	563	578	531	521	517	510	482	517	531	497	453
1055	1125	1139	1211	1293	1322	1355	1111	1082	1087	1082	1015	1156	1018	792	723
0	0	15	18	15	15	14	0	0	0	0	0	0	120	140	140
1055	1125	1154	1229	1308	1337	1369	1111	1082	1087	1082	1015	1156	1138	932	863
949	581	574	611	666	743	802	817	813	892	1093	1421	1465	1223	828	591
0	0	20	20	20	170	146	18	17	15	0	0	0	0	0	0
949	581	594	631	686	913	948	835	830	907	1093	1421	1465	1223	828	591
448	485	502	664	720	788	860	867	871	820	873	879	986	1060	1072	1076
20	40	100	30	50	35	60	0	0	0	0	0	0	0	0	0
468	525	602	694	770	823	920	867	871	820	873	879	986	1060	1072	1076
12	13	14	70	90	100	135	160	204	600	812	1102	1324	1408	1357	1352
375	430	570	591	579	762	779	745	759	424	240	270	290	310	350	370
387	443	584	661	669	862	914	905	963	1024	1052	1372	1614	1718	1707	1722
1349	1264	1278	1303	1281	1439	1392	1358	1627	2009	2095	2198	3037	2612	1991	1624
132	107	91	163	290	193	140	0	0	0	0	0	0	0	0	0
1481	1371	1369	1466	1571	1632	1532	1358	1627	2009	2095	2198	3037	2612	1991	1624
16253	15657	16303	18266	18487	20880	20909	19934	21590	25001	28663	33828	41560	40003	33054	30504
5053	4817	5539	5562	6348	6654	6260	6143	6490	6045	6421	7863	9548	8147	7540	7296
21306	20474	21842	23828	24835	27534	27169	26077	28080	31046	35084	41691	51108	48150	40594	37800

TABLE III. — MEMBERSHIP OF TRADE UNIONS IN SELECTED COUNTRIES

1910–1920[a]

(000's omitted)

Country	1910	1911	1912	1913	1914	1915	1916	1917	1918	1919	1920
Australia	302	365	433	498	523	528	546	564	582	628	684
Austria	200	200	257	253	147	112	109	211	295	772	830[d]
Belgium	139	189	231	203	203	[b]	[b]	[b]	450	750	920
Canada	120	133	160	176	166	143	160	205	249	378	374
Czecho-Slovakia	100	100	107	107	55	40	24	43	161	657	2,000[d]
Denmark	124	128	139	154	156	173	189	224	316	360	400
Finland	15	20	24	28	31	30	42	161	21	41	59
France	977	1,029	1,064	1,027	1,026	[b]	[b]	1,500	2,000	2,500	1,581[f]
Germany	2,960	3,336	3,566	3,572	2,271	1,524	1,496	1,937	3,801	9,000	13,000[d]
Hungary	86	95	102	107	107	43	55	215	500	500	343[d]
Italy	817	847	861	972	962	806	701	740	[b]	1,800	3,100
Netherlands	154	169	189	220	227	251	304	369	456	625	683
New Zealand	57	56	61	71	74	68	71	[b]	[b]	83[c]	
Norway	47	53	61	64	68	78	81	94	180	144	142
Roumania	8	6	10	[b]	[b]	17	16	16	[b]	75[c]	90
Serbia (Jugo Slavia)	7	8	5	9	14	12	12	12	15	20	[b]
Sweden	115	111	120	136	141	151	189	244	302	339	400[d]
Switzerland	75	78	86	89	50	65	89	149	177	224	292
United Kingdom	2,400	2,970	3,226	4,192	4,199	4,417	4,677	5,547	6,645	8,024	8,493[e]

[a] Unless otherwise indicated, data for the years 1910 to 1919 were taken from the International Labor Office, *Studies and Reports*, Series A, No. 17; and for 1920 from *International Labour Review*, Vol. VIII, No. 1–2, p. 79.

[b] Figures not available.

[c] From the *International Labour Review*, Vol. VIII, No. 1–2, p. 79.

[d] Based on partial information.

[e] Great Britain, *Labour Gazette*, Vol. 31, p. 383.

[f] France, *Annuaire Statistique*, 1922, p. 217.

TABLE IV.

THE WORKING POPULATION OF THE UNITED STATES, 1920 AND 1910

(Classified as Employers or Self-Employed, Supervisory Persons, and Wage Earners)

Industry	1920			1910		
	Total	Male	Female	Total	Male	Female
Extraction of Minerals	1,090,223	1,087,359	2,864	965,169	964,075	1,094
Employers	17,334	17,216	118	14,287	14,201	86
Supervisory	53,922	53,850	72	34,285	34,254	31
Foremen, Overseers, Inspectors	36,931	36,923	8	23,338	23,328	10
Managers	14,469	14,446	23	9,798	9,786	12
Officials	2,522	2,481	41	1,149	1,140	9
Wage Earners	1,018,967	1,016,293	2,674	916,597	915,620	977
Coal Mines	733,936	732,441	1,495	613,924	613,519	405
Other Mines	148,847	148,471	376	191,906	191,726	180
Copper	36,054	35,918	136	39,270	39,251	19
Gold and silver	32,700	32,666	34	55,436	55,397	39
Iron	38,704	38,605	99	49,948	49,909	39
Not specified	41,389	41,282	107	47,252	47,169	83
Quarries	45,162	45,084	78	80,840	80,795	45
Oil, Gas and Salt wells	91,022	90,297	725	29,927	29,580	347
Manufacturing Industries	9,895,105	7,982,754	1,912,351	7,517,202	5,719,016	1,798,186
Employers and Self-employed	562,199	312,035	250,164	814,974	361,693	453,281
Dressmakers	176,891	252	176,639	337,002	1,192	335,810
Milliners	54,941	2,743	52,198	95,926	4,099	91,827
Tailors and Tailoresses	96,116	80,202	15,914	102,304	81,898	20,406
Shoemakers	39,430	39,300	130	34,785	34,394	391
Piano Tuners	3,523	3,503	20	3,316	3,264	52
Jewelers, etc	7,912	7,594	318	6,534	6,037	497
Manufacturers	183,386	178,441	4,945	235,107	230,809	4,298
Supervisory	557,363	518,861	38,502	300,792	279,189	21,603
Foremen and Overseers	307,413	277,242	30,171	175,098	155,358	19,740
Managers and Superintendents	201,721	196,771	4,950	104,210	102,748	1,462
Officials	48,229	44,848	3,381	21,484	21,083	401
Wage Earners	8,775,543	7,151,858	1,623,685	6,401,436	5,078,134	1,323,302
Chemical and Allied Industries	187,291	164,640	22,651	106,334	90,533	15,801
Laborers	74,289	70,994	3,295	41,741	39,711	2,030
Semi-skilled	50,341	32,072	18,269	30,705	17,158	13,547
Charcoal and coke (laborers)	9,384	9,352	32	11,446	11,431	15
Charcoal and coke (semi-skilled)	1,722	1,692	30	1,634	1,618	16
Petroleum refineries (laborers)	31,795	31,566	229	11,215	11,151	64
Petroleum refineries (semi-skilled)	8,891	8,229	662	1,739	1,669	70
Turpentine (laborers)	9,731	9,605	126	6,405	6,354	51
Turpentine (semi-skilled)	1,138	1,130	8	1,449	1,441	8

TABLE IV. — THE WORKING POPULATION OF THE UNITED STATES, 1920 AND 1910 — *Continued*

Industry	1920			1910		
	Total	Male	Female	Total	Male	Female
Manufacturing Industries (cont.)						
Clay, Glass and Stone	241,221	223,635	17,586	294,812	282,868	11,944
Laborers	124,544	120,215	4,329	154,826	152,438	2,388
Semi-skilled	85,434	72,269	13,165	88,691	79,230	9,461
Glass blowers	9,144	9,055	89	15,564	15,474	90
Stone cutters	22,099	22,096	3	35,731	35,726	5
Clothing	599,857	231,349	368,508	655,011	237,968	417,043
Laborers	12,776	6,414	6,362	10,240	5,424	4,816
Semi-skilled	409,361	143,718	265,643	386,136	148,866	237,270
Dressmakers', etc., apprentices	4,326	17	4,309	12,011	31	11,980
Dressmakers (not in factory)	58,964	84	58,880	112,340	390	111,950
Milliners and millinery dealers	18,314	914	17,400	31,980	1,360	30,620
Tailors and tailoresses	96,116	80,202	15,914	102,304	81,897	20,407
Food	469,642	376,502	93,140	299,981	252,219	47,762
Laborers	159,535	143,397	16,138	82,015	75,691	6,324
Semi-skilled	188,895	116,493	72,402	105,283	68,683	36,600
Bakers	97,940	93,347	4,593	89,531	84,752	4,779
Millers	23,272	23,265	7	23,152	23,093	59
Cigar and Tobacco	180,379	82,557	97,822	168,193	91,392	76,801
Laborers	35,157	21,295	13,862	16,392	11,436	4,956
Semi-skilled	145,222	61,262	83,960	151,801	79,956	71,845
Liquor and Beverage	26,185	25,255	930	50,360	47,958	2,402
Laborers	10,530	10,295	235	18,857	18,294	563
Semi-skilled	15,655	14,960	695	31,503	29,664	1,839
Leather Products	373,300	283,904	89,396	323,860	255,015	68,845
Harness and saddle (laborers)	1,885	1,727	158	1,298	1,210	88
Harness and saddle (semi-skilled)	18,135	17,573	562	22,650	21,958	692
Leather belt, etc. (laborers)	3,578	3,274	304	1,908	1,757	151
Leather belt, etc. (semi-skilled)	17,189	12,809	4,380	11,553	8,473	3,080
Trunk (laborers)	2,486	2,269	217	985	909	76
Trunk (semi-skilled)	5,456	4,644	812	4,944	4,381	563
Shoe factories (laborers)	19,210	14,194	5,016	10,277	7,952	2,325
Shoe factories (semi-skilled)	206,225	132,813	73,412	181,010	121,744	59,266
Shoemakers (not in factory)	39,430	39,300	130	34,785	34,394	391
Tanneries (laborers)	27,480	26,703	777	20,798	20,491	307
Tanneries (semi-skilled)	32,226	28,598	3,628	33,652	31,746	1,906
Printing and Publishing	273,910	226,334	47,576	250,783	203,792	46,991
Printers', etc., apprentices	11,603	10,366	1,237	12,395	11,454	941
Compositors, etc	140,165	128,859	11,306	127,589	113,538	14,051
Electrotypers, etc	13,716	13,530	186	12,506	11,929	577
Engravers	15,053	14,492	561	13,967	13,429	538
Pressmen, etc	18,683	18,683	......	20,084	19,892	192
Printing, etc. (laborers)	7,981	6,240	1,741	5,484	4,121	1,363
Printing, etc. (semi-skilled)	66,709	34,164	32,545	58,758	29,429	29,329

TABLE IV. — THE WORKING POPULATION OF THE UNITED STATES, 1920 AND 1910 — *Continued*

Industry	1920			1910		
	Total	Male	Female	Total	Male	Female
Manufacturing Industries (cont.)						
Paper and Pulp Products.....	147,917	108,348	39,569	98,680	65,933	32,747
Paper and pulp mills (laborers).............	52,263	49,786	2,477	31,388	29,959	1,429
Paper and pulp mills (semi-skilled)...............	54,669	41,321	13,348	36,383	25,803	10,580
Blank book, etc. (laborers)..	3,455	2,646	809	1,557	1,096	461
Blank book, etc. (semi-skilled)...............	13,694	5,117	8,577	10,032	3,422	6,610
Paper box (laborers).......	3,384	2,401	983	1,403	791	612
Paper box (semi-skilled)....	20,452	7,077	13,375	17,917	4,862	13,055
Textile.....................	976,777	505,311	471,466	804,003	401,363	402,640
Dyers.....................	15,109	14,978	131	14,050	13,396	654
Loom fixers...............	15,961	15,958	3	13,254	13,254	......
Textile (laborers)..........	153,310	120,341	32,969	87,146	71,107	16,039
Textile (semi-skilled).......	792,397	354,034	438,363	689,553	303,606	385,947
Wood Products.............	658,262	623,217	35,045	652,845	630,812	22,033
Cabinet makers' apprentices	1,020	1,020	......	*	*	......
Coopers' apprentices.......	365	365	....	*	*	......
Cabinet makers...........	45,511	45,503	8	41,892	41,884	8
Coopers..................	19,066	19,061	5	25,299	25,292	7
Lumber, etc. (laborers).....	320,613	309,874	10,739	317,244	313,228	4,016
Lumber, etc. (semi-skilled)..	168,719	150,079	18,640	168,271	154,324	13,947
Sawyers..................	33,809	33,800	9	43,276	43,257	19
Wood carvers............	3,025	3,008	17	5,368	5,308	60
Upholsterers..............	29,605	27,338	2,267	20,221	18,928	1,293
Painters (factory)..........	17,600	17,040	560	15,230	14,950	280
Piano tuners..............	3,523	3,503	20	3,316	3,264	52
Broom and brush (laborers)	2,800	2,407	393	1,565	1,340	225
Broom and brush (semi-skilled)...............	12,606	10,219	2,387	11,163	9,037	2,126
Iron and Steel...............	3,107,082	3,034,864	72,218	2,008,006	1,976,674	31,332
Blacksmiths' apprentices...	2,661	2,659	2	2,816	2,814	2
Boilermakers' apprentices...	2,005	2,005	......	*	*	*
Machinists' apprentices....	39,463	39,448	15	*	*	*
Blacksmiths, etc...........	221,421	221,416	5	240,174	240,143	31
Boilermakers.............	74,088	74,088	......	44,761	44,761	......
Furnacemen, etc..........	40,806	40,800	6	36,251	36,226	25
Machinists, etc............	894,662	894,654	8	488,049	487,956	93
Iron molders, etc..........	114,031	114,022	9	112,122	112,070	52
Pattern makers, etc........	27,720	27,663	57	23,559	23,006	553
Rollers, etc...............	25,061	25,061	......	18,407	18,384	23
Annealers................	2,913	2,910	3	1,901	1,894	7
Laborers.................	729,613	717,022	12,591	482,941	476,801	6,140
Semi-skilled...............	689,980	632,161	57,819	369,040	345,483	23,557
Painters (factory).........	52,798	51,095	1,703	45,685	44,836	849
Carpenters...............	98,600	98,600	......	90,790	90,790	......
Electricians...............	91,260	91,260	......	51,510	51,510	......

* Figures not available.

Table IV. — The Working Population of the United States, 1920 and 1910 — *Continued*

Industry	1920			1910		
	Total	Male	Female	Total	Male	Female
Manufacturing Industries (cont.)						
Metal (except Iron and Steel)	415,396	345,001	70,395	271,221	230,346	40,875
Jewelers', etc., apprentices	2,633	2,247	386	1,839	1,770	69
Filers, grinders, etc	59,785	57,315	2,470	49,525	46,679	2,846
Jewelers, etc	31,680	30,320	1,360	26,040	24,000	2,040
Electricians	60,840	60,840	......	34,340	34,340	......
Brass and other molders	9,650	9,650	......	8,778	8,778	......
Electrical supply (laborers)	26,789	23,562	3,227	11,434	10,053	1,381
Electrical supply (semi-skilled)	64,841	37,452	27,389	24,677	13,636	11,041
Other metal (laborers)	67,887	62,771	5,116	44,773	42,134	2,639
Other metal (semi-skilled)	91,291	60,844	30,447	69,815	48,956	20,859
Miscellaneous	1,118,324	920,941	197,383	417,347	311,261	106,086
Other apprentices	47,885	44,440	3,445	*	*	*
Button factories (laborers)	1,407	1,093	314	1,105	790	315
Button factories (semi-skilled)	12,977	7,768	5,209	11,461	6,682	4,779
Gas works (laborers)	18,845	18,787	58	16,549	16,534	15
Gas works (semi-skilled)	9,462	9,294	168	5,732	5,689	43
Rubber factories (laborers)	51,467	47,515	3,952	13,546	12,224	1,322
Rubber factories (semi-skilled)	86,204	67,370	18,834	31,593	21,170	10,423
Straw factories (laborers)	577	513	64	413	319	94
Straw factories (semi-skilled)	14,102	7,751	6,351	5,915	1,945	3,970
Other miscellaneous (laborers)	84,337	77,583	6,754	32,237	29,836	2,401
Other miscellaneous (semi-skilled)	121,968	75,772	46,196	71,050	41,244	29,806
Other n. s. (laborers)	191,364	170,921	20,443	109,433	99,723	9,710
Other n. s. (semi-skilled)	207,047	121,496	85,551	104,300	61,115	43,185
Other mechanics (n. o. s.)	246,070	246,070	......	*	*	*
Oilers of machinery	24,612	24,568	44	14,013	13,990	23
Transportation	3,256,330	3,043,055	213,275	2,884,337	2,777,561	106,776
Employers and Self-employed	81,488	80,943	545	59,572	59,136	436
Captains (water transportation)	2,600	2,600	......	2,400	2,400	......
Garage keepers, etc	42,151	41,944	207	5,279	5,256	23
Livery stable keepers	11,240	11,168	72	34,795	34,612	183
Proprietors, etc. (transfer cos.)	23,497	23,231	266	15,598	15,368	230
Proprietors (n. o. s.)	2,000	2,000	......	1,500	1,500	......
Supervisory	212,228	211,102	1,126	160,091	157,741	2,350
Officials, etc. (n. o. s.)	16,957	16,384	573	13,339	11,911	1,428
Foremen, etc. (water transportation)	3,488	3,488	......	3,016	3,016	......
Foremen, etc. (livery companies)	3,868	3,866	2	6,606	6,606	......
Foremen, etc. (street railroad)	6,248	6,236	12	4,673	4,655	18

* Figures not available.

Table IV. — The Working Population of the United States, 1920 and 1910 — *Continued*

Industry	1920			1910		
	Total	Male	Female	Total	Male	Female
Transportation (cont.)						
Officials, etc. (street railroad)	3,455	3,445	10	2,433	2,433	......
Foremen (road building)	9,558	9,557	1	7,064	7,064	......
Inspectors	50,233	49,848	385	33,237	32,962	275
Foremen, etc. (steam railroad)	73,046	72,980	66	65,260	65,038	222
Officials, etc. (steam railroad)	32,426	32,385	41	19,805	19,803	2
Foremen (telegraph, etc.)	6,822	6,797	25	3,843	3,439	404
Foremen (other transportation)	6,127	6,116	11	815	814	1
Wage Earners	2,962,614	2,751,010	211,604	2,664,674	2,560,684	103,990
Water Transportation	178,539	178,127	412	152,725	152,524	201
Boatmen, etc	6,319	6,286	33	5,304	5,289	15
Captains, etc	23,720	23,720	......	21,842	21,842	......
Longshoremen, etc	85,928	85,605	323	62,857	62,813	44
Sailors and deckhands	54,832	54,800	32	46,510	46,498	12
Laborers	5,966	5,963	3	14,267	14,177	90
Semi-skilled	1,774	1,753	21	1,945	1,905	40
Road and Street Transportation	925,895	923,897	1,998	787,105	786,800	305
Carriage, etc., drivers	9,057	8,966	91	35,376	35,339	37
Chauffeurs	285,045	284,096	949	45,785	45,752	33
Draymen, etc	411,132	410,484	648	408,469	408,396	73
Hostlers, etc	18,976	18,973	3	63,388	63,382	6
Garage laborers	31,450	31,339	111	4,468	4,462	6
Deliverymen (bakeries, etc.)	170,235	170,039	196	229,619	229,469	150
Street Maintenance, etc	131,467	131,196	271	195,490	195,140	350
Laborers (road building)	115,836	115,673	163	180,468	180,468	......
Laborers (street cleaning)	11,196	11,192	4	9,946	9,946	....
Semi-skilled (road building)	4,435	4,331	104	5,076	4,726	350
Electric and Street Railways	163,992	163,076	916	148,297	148,052	245
Conductors	63,760	63,507	253	56,932	56,932	......
Laborers	25,514	25,046	468	27,807	27,602	205
Motormen	62,959	62,939	20	56,218	56,218	......
Switchmen	2,500	2,496	4	2,153	2,153	......
Semi-skilled	9,259	9,088	171	5,187	5,147	40
Steam Railroads	1,108,424	1,098,220	10,204	1,067,977	1,063,164	4,813
Baggagemen and freight agents	16,819	16,789	30	17,033	17,028	5
Boiler washers, etc	25,305	25,271	34	10,409	10,409	......
Brakemen	114,107	114,107	......	92,572	92,572	......
Conductors	74,539	74,539	......	65,604	65,604	......
Laborers	470,199	463,613	6,586	543,168	539,920	3,248
Locomotive engineers	109,899	109,899	......	96,229	96,229	......
Locomotive firemen	91,345	91,345	......	76,381	76,381	......
Motormen	3,560	3,560	......	2,487	2,487	......
Switchmen, etc	101,917	101,359	558	73,419	73,367	52
Yardmen	7,148	7,145	3	9,575	9,575	......
Ticket agents	26,585	24,324	2,261	24,138	22,930	1,208
Semi-skilled	28,621	27,916	705	24,424	24,125	299
Railway mail clerks	15,867	15,867	......	15,240	15,240	......
Railroad porters	22,513	22,486	27	17,298	17,297	1

Table IV. — The Working Population of the United States, 1920 and 1910 — *Continued*

Industry	1920			1910		
	Total	Male	Female	Total	Male	Female
Transportation (cont.)						
Express companies	23,520	23,389	131	15,666	15,561	105
Agents	5,293	5,193	100	5,875	5,804	71
Messengers	9,138	9,129	9	6,781	6,778	3
Laborers	9,089	9,067	22	3,010	2,979	31
Mail carriers	91,451	90,131	1,320	80,678	79,667	1,011
Telegraph and Telephone	323,833	127,650	196,183	211,873	115,029	96,844
Linemen	37,917	37,905	12	28,350	28,347	3
Messengers	9,403	8,969	434	9,152	9,074	78
Operators (telegraph)	79,434	62,574	16,860	69,953	61,734	8,219
Operators (telephone)	190,160	11,781	178,379	97,893	9,631	88,262
Laborers	5,088	5,011	77	5,312	5,251	61
Semi-skilled	1,831	1,410	421	1,213	992	221
Other Transportation	15,493	15,324	169	4,863	4,747	116
Laborers	5,920	5,826	94	1,361	1,288	73
Semi-skilled	2,204	2,136	68	897	854	43
Pipe-line laborers	7,369	7,362	7	2,605	2,605	......
Building Trades	2,487,500	2,470,437	17,063	2,649,751	2,630,561	19,190
Employers and Self-employed Builders and Contractors	90,109	90,030	79	174,422	173,573	849
Wage Earners	2,397,391	2,380,407	16,984	2,475,329	2,456,988	18,341
Carpenters' apprentices	4,805	4,797	8	6,069	6,061	8
Electricians' apprentices	9,562	9,557	5	2,661	2,660	1
Masons' apprentices	1,434	1,434	......	2,503	2,501	2
Painters', etc., apprentices	1,616	1,598	18	2,662	2,653	9
Paper hangers' apprentices	172	165	7	444	440	4
Plasterers' apprentices	398	398	......	669	669	......
Plumbers' apprentices	7,386	7,386	......	9,903	9,899	4
Roofers', etc., apprentices	250	250	......	304	302	2
Tinsmiths', etc., apprentices	2,816	2,815	1	*	*	*
Brick and stone masons	131,264	131,257	7	169,402	169,387	15
Carpenters	788,779	788,608	171	726,330	726,292	38
Electricians	60,840	60,840	......	34,340	34,340	......
Cranemen, etc	37,888	37,876	12	*	*	*
Building laborers	623,203	608,075	15,128	869,478	853,679	15,799
Other mechanics	27,300	27,300	......	*	....	......
Painters	252,634	251,562	1,072	276,440	275,028	1,412
Paper hangers	18,746	18,338	408	25,577	24,780	797
Plasterers and cement finishers	45,876	45,870	6	47,682	47,676	6
Plumbers, etc	206,718	206,715	3	148,304	148,304	......
Roofers and slaters	11,378	11,378	......	14,078	14,078	......
Tin and coppersmiths	74,968	74,957	11	59,833	59,809	24
Structural ironworkers	18,836	18,836	......	11,427	11,427	......
Semi-skilled	7,003	6,983	20	920	781	139
Helpers	63,519	63,412	107	66,303	66,222	81

* Figures not available.

TABLE IV. — THE WORKING POPULATION OF THE UNITED STATES, 1920 AND 1910 — *Continued*

Industry	1920			1910		
	Total	Male	Female	Total	Male	Female
Stationary Engineers	242,096	242,064	32	231,041	231,031	10
Stationary Firemen	143,875	143,862	13	111,248	111,248	......
Trade	4,248,516	3,565,089	683,427	3,490,178	3,013,438	476,740
Employers and Self-employed	1,786,902	1,690,122	96,780	1,530,340	1,454,803	75,537
Salaried	524,014	494,038	29,976	396,721	377,514	19,207
Clerks and Salespeople in Stores	1,591,412	1,059,873	531,539	1,308,313	938,999	369,314
Laborers	346,188	321,056	25,132	254,804	242,122	12,682
Professional Service	2,143,889	1,127,391	1,016,498	1,693,361	959,470	733,891
Professional	1,995,622	1,042,072	953,550	1,611,695	904,422	707,273
Semi-professional	116,555	70,626	45,929	64,926	44,532	20,394
Attendants and Helpers	31,712	14,693	17,019	16,740	10,516	6,224
Domestic and Personal Service	3,382,379	1,195,482	2,186,897	3,755,261	1,224,040	2,531,221
Employers and Self-employed	426,688	188,720	237,968	512,081	218,810	293,271
Supervisory	52,736	39,317	13,419	57,273	44,246	13,027
Wage Earners	2,902,955	967,445	1,935,510	3,185,907	960,984	2,224,923
Clerical	2,950,769	1,540,484	1,410,285	1,631,926	1,047,504	584,422
Bookkeepers, Cashiers and Accountants	734,688	375,564	359,124	486,700	299,545	187,155
Clerks (except in stores)	1,487,905	1,015,742	472,163	720,498	597,833	122,665
Messenger Boys, etc.	113,022	98,768	14,254	108,035	96,748	11,287
Stenographers and Typists	615,154	50,410	564,744	316,693	53,378	263,315
Public Service†	801,826	779,531	22,295	476,347	462,448	13,899
Agriculture, Forestry and Animal Husbandry	10,953,158	9,869,030	1,084,128	12,659,082	10,851,581	1,807,501
Employers	8,251,313	7,409,046	842,267	9,457,591	8,007,807	1,449,784
Supervisory	101,233	86,888	14,345	57,718	49,942	7,776
Wage Earners	2,600,612	2,373,096	227,516	3,143,773	2,793,832	349,941
Total for all Industries	**41,595,666**	**33,046,538**	**8,549,128**	**38,064,903**	**29,991,973**	**8,072,930**

† Not elsewhere classified.

NOTES TO TABLE IV

Unless otherwise indicated, the figures for wage earners in each industry included in table IV represent the sum of the "semi-skilled" workers and "laborers," shown by the Census to be working in that industry. The following notes indicate in detail the constitution of each item in table IV.

Extraction of Minerals.

All figures in this category are taken without change from the Census. The Census group of "oper ators" is designated in table IV as "employers."

Manufacturing Industries

Employers and self-employed.—Into this category were put the following percentages of the total number reported by the Census as working in each specified occupation: dressmakers (not in factory), 75; milliners, 75; tailors and tailoresses, 50; shoemakers (not in factory), 50; piano tuners, 50; jewelers, etc., 20.

Wage Earners:

Clothing.—Dressmakers (not in factory), 25 per cent; milliners, 25 per cent; tailors and tailoresses, 50 per cent.

Food.—Includes "laborers" and "semi-skilled" in bakeries; butter and cheese, candy, fish-curing factories; flour and grain mills; fruit and vegetable canning, slaughter and packing, sugar and other food factories.

Leather Products.—Shoemakers (not in factory), 50 per cent.

Wood Products.—Painters (in factory), 25 per cent; piano tuners, 50 per cent.

Iron and Steel.—Painters (in factory), 75 per cent; carpenters, 11 per cent; electricians, 43 per cent.

Metal (except Iron and Steel).—Jewelers, 80 per cent; electricians, 29 per cent.

Transportation.

Employers and self-employed.—Captains (water transportation), 10 per cent.

Wage Earners.—Captains (water transportation), 90 per cent.

Building Trades.

Wage Earners.—Painters includes "painters, glaziers and varnishers (building)" and "enamelers, lacquerers, and japanners"; carpenters, 88 per cent; electricians, 28 per cent; "other mechanics," 10 per cent.

Trade.

Employers and self-employed.—Includes bankers and brokers; insurance officials; proprietors, officials and managers; real estate agents; retail dealers; undertakers; wholesale dealers, etc.

Salaried.—Includes commercial travelers; decorators, etc.; floorwalkers, etc.; inspectors, etc.; insurance agents; agents, canvassers, and collectors.

Domestic and Personal Service.

Employers and self-employed.—Barbers, 20 per cent; billiard room, etc., keepers; boarding house keepers; hotel keepers and managers, 20 per cent; launderers (not in factory), 25 per cent; laundry owners; restaurant keepers; saloon keepers.

Supervisory.—Laundry foremen; laundry managers; hotel keepers and managers, 80 per cent.

Public Service.

Includes "public service (not elsewhere classified)," "laborers" and "semi-skilled" in electric light and power plants.

Agriculture.

Employers and self-employed.—Includes dairy farmers, etc.; farm laborers (home farm); fishermen and oystermen, 10 per cent; gardeners, etc., owners, lumber camps; apiarists; corn shellers, 20 per cent; poultry raisers.

Supervisory.—Includes farm foremen; lumber foremen; managers, timber camps.

TABLE V.—MEMBERSHIP OF AMERICAN TRADE UNIONS IN THE UNITED STATES AND CANADA, BY SEX, 1920

(00's omitted)

(UNLESS OTHERWISE SPECIFIED, THE DATA IN THIS TABLE WERE OBTAINED EITHER FROM THE PROCEEDINGS OR OFFICERS' REPORTS OR BY CORRESPONDENCE WITH THE CENTRAL OFFICE OF THE UNION)

Name of Union	Total	Total Male	Total Female	Canadian[b]	U. S.[c]	U. S. Male	U. S. Female[c]
Actors	90	51	39	....	90	51	39
Asbestos Workers	22[a]	22	....	1	21	21	....
Automobile, Aircraft Workers	454	454	....	....	454	454	....
Bakery Workers	275[a]	275	....	6	269	269	....
Barbers	442[a]	442	....	15	427	427	....
Bill Posters	16[a]	16	....	1	15	15	....
Blacksmiths	483[a]	483	....	18	465	465	....
Boilermakers and Iron Shipbuilders	1030[a]	1030	....	58	972	972	....
Bookbinders	207[a]	115	92	18	189	105	84
Boot and Shoe Workers	467[a]	317	150	30	437	297	140
Brewery Workers	341[a]	339	2	8	333	331	2
Brick and Tile Workers	52[a]	52	....	....	52	52	....
Bricklayers and Masons	736	736	....	41	695	695	....
Bridge and Iron Workers	277	277	....	37	240	240	....
Broom Makers	14[a]	14	....	....	14	14	....
Carpenters	3719	3719	....	167	3552	3552	....
Cigarmakers	388[a]	318	70	14	374	307	67
Cloth Hat and Cap Makers	106	81	25	5	101	77	24
Clothing, Amalgamated	1770	1070	700	98	1672	1011	661
Commercial Telegraphers	50[b]	50	....	21	29[b]	29	....
Coopers	43[a]	43	....	....	43	43	....
Cutting Die Makers	2[a]	2	....	....	2	2	....
Diamond Workers	6[a]	6	....	....	6	6	....
Draftsmen	35[a]	35	....	....	35	35	....
Elastic Goring Weavers	1[a]	1	....	....	1	1	....
Electrical Workers	1392[a]	1252	140	46	1346	1211	135
Elevator Constructors	31[a]	31	....	1	30	30	....
Federal Employees	385[a]	385	....	2	383	383	....
Fire Fighters	221[a]	221	....	18	203	203	....
Flint Glass Workers	99[a]	99	....	3	96	96	....
Foundry Employees	91[a]	91	....	....	91	91	....
Fur Workers	121[a]	85	36	10	111	78	33
Garment Workers, United	459[a]	139	320	13	446	135	311
Glass Bottle Blowers	100[a]	100	....	3	97	97	....
Glove Workers	10[a]	3	7	1	9	3	6
Granite Cutters	115	115	....	3	112	112	...

TABLE V. — MEMBERSHIP OF AMERICAN TRADE UNIONS IN THE UNITED STATES AND CANADA, BY SEX, 1920 — *Continued*

(00's omitted)

Name of Union	Total	Total Male	Total Female	Canadian[b]	U. S.[c]	U. S. Male	U. S. Female[g]
Hatters	105[a]	85	20	....	105	85	20
Hod Carriers	420[a]	420	....	13	407	407	....
Horse Shoers	54[a]	54	....	....	54	54	....
Hotel Employees	604[a]	548	56	21	583	529	54
Iron, Steel and Tin Workers	315[a]	315	....	21	294	294	....
Jewelry Workers	81[a]	81	....	10	71	71	....
Lace Operatives	9[d]	9	....	....	9	9	....
Ladies' Garment Workers	1054[a]	377	677	37	1017	364	653
Lathers, Wood and Metal	59[a]	59	....	2	57	57	....
Laundry Workers	80[a]	18	62	....	80	18	62
Leather Goods Workers, Fancy	35	33	2	....	35	33	2
Leather Workers	117[a]	87	30[e]	3	114	85	29
Letter Carriers	224	224	....	....	224	224	....
Letter Carriers, Rural	3[a]	3	....	....	3	3	....
Lithographers	61[a]	61	....	5	56	56	....
Locomotive Engineers	869	869	....	65	804	804	....
Locomotive Firemen	1259	1259	....	88	1171	1171	....
Longshoremen	740[a]	740	....	37	703	703	....
Machine Printers	5[a]	5	....	....	5	5	....
Machinists	3308[a]	3303	5	141	3167	3162	5
Maintenance of Way Employees	1560[b]	1560[b]	....	114	1446[b]	1446[b]	....
Marble Workers	12[a]	12	....	....	12	12	....
Marine Engineers	170[a]	170	....	....	170	170	....
Masters, Mates and Pilots	71[a]	71	....	4	67	67	....
Meat Cutters	653[a]	599	54[e]	20	633	581	52
Metal Polishers	125	125	....	3	122	122	....
Mine, Mill, and Smelter Workers	211[a]	211	....	4	207	207	....
Mine Workers, United	3936[a]	3936	....	198	3738	3738	....
Molders	573[a]	573	....	36	537	537	....
Musicians	700[a]	672	28	50	650	624	26
Oil and Gas Well Workers	209[a]	209	....	....	209	209	....
Painters	1031[a]	1031	....	31	1000	1000	....
Paper Makers	74[a]	74	....	11	63	63	....
Pattern Makers	90[a]	90	....	6	84	84	....
Pavers	19[a]	19	....	1	18	18	....
Paving Cutters	26[a]	26	....	1	25	25	....
Photo Engravers	59[a]	59	....	4	55	55	....
Piano and Organ Workers	32[a]	32	....	3	29	29	....
Plasterers	194[a]	194	....	14	180	180	....
Plumbers	750	750	....	33	717	717	....

TABLE V. — MEMBERSHIP OF AMERICAN TRADE UNIONS IN THE UNITED STATES AND CANADA, BY SEX, 1920 — *Continued*

(00's omitted)

Name of Union	Total	Total Male	Total Female	Canadian[b]	U. S.[c]	U. S. Male	U. S. Female[c]
Poster Artists	4	4	....	....	4	4	....
Post Office Clerks, Natl	250	220	30	....	250	220	30
Post Office Clerks, United	290	264	26	....	290	264	26
Potters, Operative	80[a]	65	15	....	80	65	15
Powder Workers	3[a]	3	....	....	3	3	....
Print Cutters	4[a]	4	....	....	4	4	....
Printing Pressmen	350[a]	335	15	6	344	329	15
Pulp and Paper Mill Workers	95[a]	85	10[e]	50	45	40	5
Quarry Workers	30[a]	30	....	4	26	26	....
Railroad Patrolmen	26[a]	26	....	....	26	26	....
Railroad Signalmen	123[a]	123	....	2	121	121	....
Railroad Station Agents	88	88	....	....	88	88	....
Railroad Stationmen	33	33	....	17	16	16	....
Railroad Station Employees	352	352	....	....	352	352	....
Railroad Telegraphers	780	755	25	102	678	656	22
Railroad Trainmen	1846	1846	....	142	1704	1704	....
Railway Carmen	1821[a]	1821	....	145	1676	1676	....
Railway Clerks	1860[a]	1510	350	100	1760	1430	330
Railway Conductors	560	560	....	35	525	525	....
Railway Mail Association	148	148	....	....	148	148	....
Retail Clerks	208[a]	179	29[f]	4	204	175	29
Roofers, Composition	18[a]	18	....	1	17	17	....
Saw Smiths	1[a]	1	....	....	1	1	....
Seamen	659[a]	659	....	20	639	639	....
Silk Workers	10	10	....	....	10	10	....
Sleeping Car Conductors	12[a]	12	....	....	12	12	....
Sheet Metal Workers	218[a]	218	....	9	209	209	....
Shoe Workers' Protective	180	100	80	....	180	100	80
Shoe Workers, United	330	200	130	....	330	200	130
Spinners	22	22	....	....	22	22	....
Stationary Firemen	296[a]	296	....	10	286	286	....
Steam Engineers	320[a]	320	....	20	300	300	....
Steam Shovelmen	80	80	....	14	66	66	....
Steel Plate Engravers	2[a]	2	....	....	2	2	....
Steel Plate Printers	14[a]	14	....	....	14	14	....
Steel Plate Transferers	1[a]	1	....	....	1	1	....
Stereotypers	59[a]	59	....	2	57	57	....
Stone Cutters	40[a]	40	....	8	32	32	....
Stove Mounters	19[a]	19	....	2	17	17	....
Street and Electric Railway Employees	987[a]	987	....	119	868	868	....
Switchmen	140[a]	140	....	1	139	139	....

Table V. — Membership of American Trade Unions in the United States and Canada, by Sex, 1920 — *Continued*

(00's omitted)

Name of Union	Total	Total Male	Total Female	Canadian[b]	U. S.[c]	U. S. Male	U. S. Female[g]
Tailors	120[a]	100	20	5	115	96	19
Teachers, Amer. Fed. of	87[a]	35	52	1	86	34	52
Teamsters and Chauffeurs	1108[a]	1108	....	7	1101	1101	....
Textile Workers, Amalgamated	400	250	150	....	400	250	150
Textile Workers, United	1049[a]	649	400	25	1024	634	390
Theatrical Stage Employees	196[a]	196	....	5	191	191	....
Timber Workers	101[a]	101	....	1	100	100	....
Tobacco Workers	152[a]	87	65	....	152	87	65
Trade and Federal Unions	868[a]	868	....	24	844	844	....
Tunnel Constructors	30[a]	30	....	....	30	30	....
Typographical Union	705[a]	683	22	54	651	631	20
Upholsterers	56[a]	56	....	1	55	55	....
Vaudeville Artists	100	65	35	....	100	65	35
Window Glass Workers	38	38	....	....	38	38	....
Wire Weavers	4[a]	4	....	....	4	4	....
Wood Carvers	12[a]	12	....	....	12	12	....
Workers' International Industrial Union	30[b]	30	....	....	30	30	....
Total	51362	47393	3969	2550	48812	44994	3818

NOTES TO TABLE V

[a] American Federation of Labor, *Annual Proceedings.*

[b] Canada, Department of Labour, *Tenth Annual Report on Labour Organization in Canada*, pp. 254–5.

[c] The data in this column were obtained by subtracting from the total membership of each organization its Canadian membership.

[d] Estimated.

[e] International Labour Office (Geneva), *International Labour Directory*, 1922, p. 584.

[f] Estimated as same per cent of total membership as in 1910.

[g] No data are available for the female Canadian membership of American unions. It was assumed, in obtaining the figures in this column, that the proportion of female members in Canada was the same as the proportion of total members.

TABLE VI. — EXTENT OF ORGANIZATION AMONG PERSONS TEN YEARS OF AGE AND OVER ENGAGED IN EACH SPECIFIED OCCUPATION IN EACH INDUSTRY OR SERVICE GROUP, 1920.

CLASSIFIED BY SEX

Name of Industry or Occupation	Number of Wage Earners in Industry or Occupation			Number of Members of Trade Unions in Industry or Occupation			Name of Organization	Percentage Organized		
	Total	Male	Female	Total	Male	Female		Total	Male	Female
Extraction of Minerals	1,018,967	1,016,293	2,674	418,000	418,000	......		41.0	41.1	....
Coal mines	733,936	732,441	1,495	373,800	373,800	......	United Mine Workers	50.9	51.0	....
Copper, gold and silver, iron, lead and zinc, other specified and not specified mines	148,847	148,471	376	20,700	20,700	......	Mine, Mill and Smelter Workers	13.9	13.9	....
Quarries	45,162	45,084	78	2,600	2,600	......	Quarry Workers	5.8	5.8	....
Production of Salt, Oil and Natural Gas	91,022	90,297	725	20,900	20,900	......	Oil and Gas Well Workers	23.0	23.1	....
Manufacturing	8,775,543	7,151,858	1,623,685	2,035,500	1,737,700	297,800		23.2	24.3	18.3
Chemical and Allied Industries	187,291	164,640	22,651	300	300	......		0.2	0.2	....
Charcoal and coke works	11,106	11,044	62	....	....	......				
Fertilizer factories	14,350	14,160	190	....	....	......				
Oil refineries	40,686	39,795	891	....	....	......				
Paint factories	10,362	9,363	999	....	....	......				
Powder, cartridge, dynamite, fuse and fireworks factories	15,846	12,632	3,214	300	300	......	Powder Workers	1.9	2.4	....
Soap factories, turpentine distilleries and other chemical factories	94,941	77,646	17,295	....	....	......				

TABLE VI. — EXTENT OF ORGANIZATION AMONG PERSONS TEN YEARS OF AGE AND OVER, 1920 — *Continued*

Name of Industry or Occupation	Number of Wage Earners in Industry or Occupation			Number of Members of Trade Unions in Industry or Occupation			Name of Organization	Percentage Organized		
	Total	Male	Female	Total	Male	Female		Total	Male	Female
Manufacturing (continued)										
Clay, Glass and Stone Industries	241,221	223,635	17,586	51,900	50,400	1,500		21.5	22.5	8.5
Brick, tile and terra cotta factories	58,623	57,456	1,167	5,200	5,200	......	Brick and Tile Workers	8.9	9.1	....
Glass factories	82,912	73,152	9,760	23,100	23,100	......		27.9	31.6	....
				9,600	9,600	......	Flint Glass Workers			
				9,700	9,700	......	Glass Bottle Blowers			
				3,800	3,800	......	Window Glass Workers			
Lime, cement and gypsum factories	37,684	37,310	374							
Marble and stone yards	32,729	32,635	94	15,600	15,600	......		47.7	47.8	....
				11,200	11,200	......	Granite Cutters			
				1,200	1,200	......	Marble Workers			
				3,200	3,200	......	Stone Cutters			
Potteries	29,273	23,082	6,191	8,000	6,500	1,500	Potters, Operative	27.3	28.2	24.2
Clothing Industries	599,857	231,349	368,508	346,500	177,100	169,400		57.8	76.6	46.0
				10,100	7,700	2,400	Cloth, Hat and Cap Makers			
				167,200	101,100	66,100	Clothing Workers, Amal.			
				44,600	13,500	31,100	Garment Workers, United			
				900	300	600	Glove Workers			
				10,500	8,500	2,000	Hatters, United			
				101,700	36,400	65,300	Ladies' Garment Workers			
				11,500	9,600	1,900	Tailors, Journeymen			
Food and Kindred Products	469,642	376,502	93,140	91,200	86,000	5,200		19.4	22.8	5.6
Bakeries	126,696	109,074	17,622	26,900	26,900	......	Bakery Workers	21.2	24.7	....
Butter and cheese factories	34,031	30,270	3,761							

Candy factories	58,865	25,311	33,554							
Fish curing and packing	13,886	9,624	4,262							
Flour and grain mills	49,505	48,772	733	1,000	1,000	......	Brewery Workers	2.0	2.1	....
Fruit and vegetable canning	23,262	13,641	9,621							
Slaughter and packing houses	109,539	97,342	12,197	63,300	58,100	5,200	Meat Cutters, Amal	57.8	59.7	42.6
Sugar factories and refineries	19,539	18,558	981							
Other food factories	34,319	23,910	10,409							
Iron and Steel Industries	3,107,082	3,034,864	72,218	872,700	872,200	500		28.1	28.7	0.7
				45,400	45,400	......	Automobile, Aircraft Workers			
				46,500	46,500	......	Blacksmiths			
				97,200	97,200	......	Boilermakers			
				29,600	29,600	......	Carpenters			
				200	200	......	Cutting Die Makers			
				50,700	50,700	......	Electrical Workers			
				9,100	9,100	......	Foundry Employees			
				29,400	29,400	......	Iron, Steel and Tin Workers			
				316,700	316,200	500	Machinists			
				53,700	53,700	......	Molders			
				16,000	16,000	......	Painters			
				8,400	8,400	......	Pattern Makers			
				167,600	167,600	......	Railway Carmen			
				100	100	......	Saw Smiths			
				1,700	1,700	......	Stove Mounters			
				400	400	......	Wire Weavers			
Leather Industries	373,300	283,904	89,396	109,700	71,600	38,100		29.4	25.2	42.6
Shoe factories	264,865	186,307	78,558	94,800	59,800	35,000		35.8	32.1	44.6
				43,700	29,700	14,000	Boot and Shoe Workers			
				100	100	......	Elastic Goring Weavers			
				18,000	10,000	8,000	Shoe Workers, Protective			
				33,000	20,000	13,000	Shoe Workers, United			

Table VI. — Extent of Organization among Persons Ten Years of Age and Over, 1920 — *Continued*

Name of Industry or Occupation	Number of Wage Earners in Industry or Occupation			Number of Members of Trade Unions in Industry or Occupation			Name of Organization	Percentage Organized		
	Total	Male	Female	Total	Male	Female		Total	Male	Female
Manufacturing (continued)										
Other Leather	108,435	97,597	10,838	14,900	11,800	3,100		13.7	12.1	28.6
				11,400	8,500	2,900	Leather Workers			
				3,500	3,300	200	Leather Goods Workers, Fancy			
Liquor and Beverage Industries	26,185	25,255	930	32,300	32,100	200	Brewery Workers			21.5
Lumber and Furniture Industries	642,856	610,591	32,265	116,600	116,600	......		18.1	19.1	....
				4,300	4,300	......	Coopers			
				88,700	88,700	......	Carpenters			
				4,000	4,000	......	Painters			
				2,900	2,900	......	Piano and Organ Workers			
				10,000	10,000	......	Timber Workers			
				5,500	5,500	......	Upholsterers			
				1,200	1,200	......	Wood Carvers			
Metal Industries (except Iron and Steel)	415,396	345,001	70,395	53,700	53,700	......		12.9	15.6	....
				600	600	......	Diamond Workers			
				33,800	33,800	......	Electrical Workers			
				7,100	7,100	......	Jewelry Workers			
				12,200	12,200	......	Metal Polishers			
Paper and Pulp Industries	147,917	108,348	39,569	11,700	11,200	500		7.9	10.3	1.3
				500	500	......	Machine Printers			
				6,300	6,300	......	Paper Makers			
				400	400	......	Print Cutters			
				4,500	4,000	500	Pulp and Paper Mill Workers			

Printing and Publishing	273,910	226,334	**47,576**	137,300	125,400	11,900		50.1	55.4	**25.0**
				18,900	10,500	8,400	Bookbinders			
				5,600	5,600	......	Lithographers			
				5,500	5,500	......	Photo Engravers			
				400	400	......	Poster Artists			
				34,400	32,900	1,500	Printing Pressmen			
				200	200	......	Steel Plate Engravers			
				1,400	1,400	......	Steel Plate Printers			
				100	100	......	Steel Plate Transferers			
				5,700	5,700	......	Stereotypers			
				65,100	63,100	2,000	Typographical Union			
Textile Industries	976,777	505,311	**471,466**	146,500	92,500	54,000		15.0	18.3	**11.5**
				900	900	......	Lace Operatives			
				1,000	1,000	......	Silk Workers			
				2,200	2,200	......	Spinners			
				40,000	25,000	15,000	Textile Workers, Amalgamated			
				102,400	63,400	39,000	Textile Workers, United			
Miscellaneous Industries										
Broom and brush factories	15,406	12,626	2,780	1,400	1,400	......	Broom Makers	9.1	11.1	....
Button factories	14,384	8,861	5,523							
Cigar and tobacco factories	180,379	82,557	97,822	52,600	39,400	13,200		29.2	47.7	13.5
				37,400	30,700	6,700	Cigarmakers			
				15,200	8,700	6,500	Tobacco Workers			
Gas Works	28,307	28,081	226							
Rubber factories	137,671	114,885	22,786							
Straw factories	14,679	8,264	6,415							
Other miscellaneous and not specified industries	923,283	760,850	162,433	11,100	7,800	3,300	Fur Workers	1.2	1.0	2.0

TABLE VI. — EXTENT OF ORGANIZATION AMONG PERSONS TEN YEARS OF AGE AND OVER, 1920 — *Continued*

Name of Industry or Occupation	Number of Wage Earners in Industry or Occupation			Number of Members of Trade Unions in Industry or Occupation			Name of Organization	Percentage Organized		
	Total	Male	Female	Total	Male	Female		Total	Male	Female
Transportation	2,985,804	2,774,153	211,651	1,113,800	1,100,000	13,800		37.3	39.7	6.5
Water transportation	184,627	184,213	414	157,900	157,900	......		85.5	85.7	....
				70,300	70,300	......	Longshoremen			
				17,000	17,000	......	Marine Engineers			
				6,700	6,700	......	Masters, Mates and Pilots			
				63,900	63,900	......	Seamen			
Construction and maintenance of streets, roads, sewers and bridges	131,467	131,196	271	10,900	10,900	......		8.3	8.3	....
				1,800	1,800	......	Pavers			
				2,500	2,500	......	Paving Cutters			
				6,600	6,600	......	Steam Shovelmen			
Electric and street railways	163,992	163,076	916	86,800	86,800	......	Street Railway Employees	52.9	53.2	....
Teamsters and chauffeurs	925,895	923,897	1,998	110,100	110,100	......	Teamsters and Chauffeurs	11.9	11.9	....
Steam railroads	1,119,411	1,109,161	10,250	643,400	643,400	......		57.5	58.0	....
				80,400	80,400	......	Locomotive Engineers			
				117,100	117,100	......	Locomotive Firemen			
				144,600	144,600	......	Maintenance of Way Employees			
				2,600	2,600	......	Railroad Patrolmen			
				12,100	12,100	......	Railroad Signalmen			
				8,800	8,800	......	Railroad Station Agents			
				1,600	1,600	......	Railroad Stationmen			
				35,200	35,200	......	Railroad Station Employees			

				170,400	170,400	......	Railroad Trainmen			
				52,500	52,500	......	Railway Conductors			
				1,200	1,200	......	Sleeping Car Conductors			
				13,900	13,900	......	Switchmen			
				3,000	3,000	......	Tunnel Constructors			
Express companies	23,520	23,389	131							
Post	91,451	90,131	1,320	22,700	22,700	......		24.8	25.2	....
				22,400	22,400	......	Letter Carriers			
				300	300	......	Letter Carriers, Rural			
Telegraph and telephone	323,821	127,650	196,171	82,300	68,500	13,800		25.4	53.7	7.0
				2,900	2,900	......	Commercial Telegraphers			
				11,600	....	11,600	Electrical Workers			
				67,800	65,600	2,200	Railroad Telegraphers			
Other and not specified transportation	21,620	21,440	180							
Building Trades	2,397,391	2,380,407	16,984	611,600	611,600	......		25.5	25.7	....
				2,100	2,100	......	Asbestos Workers			
				69,500	69,500	......	Bricklayers and Masons			
				24,000	24,000	......	Bridge and Iron Workers			
				237,700	237,700	......	Carpenters			
				36,600	36,600	......	Electrical Workers			
				3,000	3,000	......	Elevator Constructors			
				40,700	40,700	......	Hod Carriers			
				5.700	5,700	......	Lathers			
				80,000	80,000	......	Painters			
				18,000	18,000	......	Plasterers			
				71,700	71,700	......	Plumbers			
				1,700	1,700	......	Roofers, Composition			
				20,900	20,900	......	Sheet Metal Workers			
Stationary Engineers	242,096	242,064	32	30,000	30,000	......	Steam Engineers	12.4	12.4	....
Stationary Firemen	143,875	143,862	13	28,600	28,600	......	Stationary Firemen	19.9	19.9	....

TABLE VI. — EXTENT OF ORGANIZATION AMONG PERSONS TEN YEARS OF AGE AND OVER, 1920 — *Continued*

Name of Industry or Occupation	Number of Wage Earners in Industry or Occupation			Number of Members of Trade Unions in Industry or Occupation			Name of Organization	Percentage Organized		
	Total	Male	Female	Total	Male	Female		Total	Male	Female
Trade	1,937,600	1,380,929	556,671	20,400	17,500	2,900		1.1	1.3	0.5
Clerks and salespeople in stores	1,591,412	1,059,873	531,539	20,400	17,500	2,900	Retail Clerks	1.3	1.7	0.5
Laborers	346,188	321,056	25,132							
Professional Service	2,143,889	1,127,391	1,016,498	115,200	100,000	15,200		5.4	8.9	1.5
Professional	1,995,622	1,042,072	953,550	96,100	80,900	15,200		4.8	7.8	1.6
				9,000	5,100	3,900	Actors			
				3,500	3,500	......	Draftsmen			
				65,000	62,400	2,600	Musicians			
				8,600	3,400	5,200	Teachers, Amer. Fed			
				10,000	6,500	3,500	Vaudeville Artists			
Semi-professional	116,555	70,626	45,929							
Attendants and Helpers	31,712	14,693	17,019	19,100	19,100	......	Theatrical Stage Employees			
Domestic and Personal Service										
Wage Earners	2,902,955	967,445	1,935,510	109,000	97,400	11,600		3.8	10.1	0.6
				42,700	42,700	......	Barbers			
				58,300	52,900	5,400	Hotel Employees			
				8,000	1,800	6,200	Laundry Workers			
Clerical Groups	2,966,616	1,556,351	1,410,265	244,800	206,200	38,600		8.3	13.2	2.7
Bookkeepers, cashiers and accountants	734,688	375,564	359,124							
Clerks (except in stores)	1,503,772	1,031,609	472,163	244,800	206,200	38,600		16.3	20.0	8.2
				25,000	22,000	3,000	Post Office Clerks, Nat			
				29,000	26,400	2,600	Post Office Clerks, Utd			
				176,000	143,000	33,000	Railway Clerks			
				14,800	14,800	......	Railway Mail Association			

Messenger boys, etc.	113,022	98,768	14,254							
Stenographers and typists	615,154	50,410	564,744							
Public Service*	801,826	779,531	22,295	58,600	58,600	......		7.3	7.5	....
				38,300	38,300	......	Federal Employees			
				20,300	20,300	......	Fire Fighters			
Agriculture, Forestry and Animal Husbandry Wage Earners	2,600,612	2,373,096	227,516							

* (not elsewhere classified)

NOTES TO TABLE VI

The statistics for wage earners in table VI are the same as those of table IV. Where there are differences they are due to the inclusion of items in table VI, not included in the same categories in table IV. The following notes explain the differences where they exist.

Manufacturing.

Lumber and Furniture.—Excludes broom and brush factories which in this table are included in the group of miscellaneous industries.

Transportation.

Water Transportation.—This table includes 2,600 captains and 3,488 foremen, not included under wage earners, in table IV.

Steam Railroads.—Includes 42,721 inspectors, not included under wage earners, in table IV. Does not include railway mail clerks, who are included under steam transportation in table IV.

Other Transportation.—Includes 6,127 foremen and overseers, not included under wage earners, in table IV.

Clerical.

Includes railway mail clerks, not included in this category in table IV.

TABLE VII. — EXTENT OF ORGANIZATION AMONG PERSONS TEN YEARS OF AGE AND OVER ENGAGED IN EACH SPECIFIED OCCUPATION IN EACH INDUSTRY OR SERVICE GROUP, 1910

CLASSIFIED BY SEX

Name of Industry or Occupation	Number of Wage Earners in Industry or Occupation			Number of Members of Trade Unions in Industry or Occupation			Name of Organization	Percentage Organized		
	Total	Male	Female	Total	Male	Female		Total	Male	Female
Extraction of Minerals	957,851	956,870	981	261,088	261,088	......		27.3	27.3	....
Coal Mines	640,581	640,176	405	226,228	226,228	......		35.3	35.3	....
				200	200	......	I. W. W. (Chicago)			
				226,028	226,028	......	United Mine Workers			
Copper, gold and silver, iron, lead and zinc, other specified and not specified mines	193,875	193,695	180	28,551	28,551	......	West. Fed. of Miners	14.7	14.7	....
Quarries	85,919	85,874	45	6,309	6,309	......		7.3	7.3	....
				9	9	......	A. F. of L., local unions			
				1,400	1,400	......	Slate Workers			
				4,900	4,900	......	Quarry Workers			
Production of Salt, Oil and Natural Gas	37,476	37,125	351							
Manufacturing	6,261,202	5,076,989	1,184,213	724,859	663,735	61,124		11.6	13.1	5.2
Chemical and Allied Industries	119,430	103,564	15,866	1,618	1,518	100		1.4	1.5	0.6
Charcoal and Coke Works	23,294	23,259	35	1,350	1,350	......		5.8	5.8	....
				500	500	......	United Mine Workers			
				850	850	......	A. F. of L., local unions			
Fertilizer factories	10,525	10,422	103							
Oil refineries	14,653	14,513	140							
Paint factories	7,013	6,264	749							

Powder, cartridge, dynamite, fuse and fireworks factories	9,559	6,822	2,737	238	138	100	Powder Workers	2.5	2.0	3.7
Soap factories, turpentine distilleries, and other chemical factories	54,386	42,284	12,102	30	30	......	A. F. of L., local unions	0.0	0.0	....
Clay, Glass and Stone Industries.	309,341	297,284	12,057	63,416	63,318	98		20.5	21.3	0.8
Brick, tile and terra cotta factories	98,547	97,164	1,383	3,800	3,800	......	Brick Workers	3.9	3.9	....
Glass factories	83,641	78,595	5,046	28,619	28,619	......		34.2	36.4	....
				8,729	8,729	......	Flint Glass Workers			
				9,685	9,685	......	Glass Bottle Blowers			
				1,405	1,405	......	Glass Workers			
				1,800	1,800	......	Window Glass Snappers			
				7,000	7,000	......	Window Glass Workers			
Lime, cement and gypsum factories	45,226	44,945	281							
Marble and stone yards	55,558	55,334	224	25,217	25,217	......		45.4	45.6	....
				13,113	13,113	......	Granite Cutters			
				2,458	2,458	......	Marble Workers			
				171	171	......	Sculptors and Carvers, N.Y.			
				8,356	8,356	......	Stone Cutters			
				800	800	......	Stone Cutters, Nat. Soc			
				200	200	......	Stone Cutters, Soc., N. Y.			
				119	119	......	A. F. of L., local unions			
Potteries	26,369	21,246	5,123	5,780	5,682	98		21.9	26.7	1.9
				5,680	5,582	98	Potters			
				100	100	......	A. F. of L., local unions			
Clothing Industries	608,892	324,749	284,143	102,972	71,163	31,809		16.9	21.9	11.2
				875	875	......	A. F. of L., local unions			
				1,466	1,307	159	Cap Makers			
				52,665	33,232	19,433	Garment Workers, United			
				800	435	365	Glove Workers			

TABLE VII. — EXTENT OF ORGANIZATION AMONG PERSONS TEN YEARS OF AGE AND OVER, 1910 — *Continued*

Name of Industry or Occupation	Number of Wage Earners in Industry or Occupation			Number of Members of Trade Unions in Industry or Occupation			Name of Organization	Percentage Organized		
	Total	Male	Female	Total	Male	Female		Total	Male	Female
Manufacturing (continued)										
				10,334	10,334	......	Hatters			
				300	300	......	I. W. W. (Detroit)			
				25,999	14,877	11,122	Ladies' Garment Workers			
				10,533	9,803	730	Tailors			
Food and Kindred Products	299,176	252,618	46,558	22,744	22,744	......		7.6	9.0	....
Bakeries	105,599	94,028	11,571	18,410	18,410	......	Bakery Workers	17.4	19.6	....
Butter and cheese factories	16,558	15,896	662							
Candy factories	34,391	15,887	18,504							
Fish curing and packing	7,694	6,471	1,223							
Flour and grain mills	36,425	36,029	396	300	300	......	Flour Mill Employees	0.8	0.8	....
Fruit and vegetable canning	10,011	5,858	4,153							
Slaughter and packing houses	61,417	57,548	3,869	3,859	3,859	......		6.3	6.7	....
				1,784	1,784	......	Meat Cutters			
				1,975	1,975	......	Butcher Workmen			
				100	100	......	I. W. W. (Chicago)			
Sugar factories and refineries	10,890	10,565	325	175	175	......	A. F. of L., local unions	1.6	1.7	....
Other food factories	16,191	10,336	5,855							
Iron and Steel Industries	1,796,387	1,768,140	28,247	186,169	186,169	......		10.4	10.5	....
				46,438	46,438	......	Molders			
				6,423	6,423	......	Metal Polishers			
				5,500	5,500	......	Iron, Steel and Tin Workers			
				1,100	1,100	......	Carriage Workers			
				5,000	5,000	......	Car Workers			
				15,000	15,000	......	Electrical Workers			

				20,525	20,525	......	Railway Carmen...........			
				886	886	......	Shipwrights..............			
				13,051	13,051	......	Boilermakers.............			
				1,260	1,260	......	Metal Workers............			
				51,900	51,900	......	Machinists...............			
				400	400	......	Wire Weavers.............			
				9,000	9,000	......	Blacksmiths..............			
				935	935	......	Stove Mounters...........			
				700	700	......	Foundry Employees........			
				5,450	5,450	......	Pattern Makers...........			
				140	140	......	Metal Spinners of N. Y....			
				300	300	......	Cutter Makers............			
				600	600	......	I. W. W. (Detroit).........			
				300	300	......	I. W. W. (Chicago)........			
				1,261	1,261	......	A. F. of L., local unions....			
Leather Industries.............	293,035	224,368	68,667	42,644	37,121	5,523		**14.6**	**16.5**	**8.0**
Shoe factories...............	193,474	131,709	61,765	37,663	32,163	5,500		**19.5**	**24.4**	**8.9**
				30,727	25,527	5,200	Boot and Shoe Workers....			
				2,200	2,200	......	Boot and Shoe Cutters.....			
				100	100	......	Elastic Goring Weavers.....			
				4,636	4,336	300	Shoe Workers, United......			
Other leather...............	99,561	92,659	6,902	4,981	4,958	23		**5.0**	**5.4**	**0.3**
				800	800	......	Leather Workers...........			
				3,620	3,620	......	Leather Workers, Horse Goods.................			
				561	538	23	Travelers' Goods Workers...			
Liquor and Beverage Industries.	73,475	71,068	2,407	49,665	49,078	587		**67.6**	**69.1**	**24.4**
				49,419	48,832	587	Brewery Workers..........			
				246	246	......	A. F. of L., local unions....			
Lumber and Furniture Industries	622,466	603,284	19,182	63,934	63,534	400		**10.3**	**10.5**	**2.1**
				10,000	9,600	400	Box Makers...............			
				38,958	38,958	......	Carpenters, United.........			

TABLE VII. — EXTENT OF ORGANIZATION AMONG PERSONS TEN YEARS OF AGE AND OVER, 1910 — *Continued*

Name of Industry or Occupation	Number of Wage Earners in Industry or Occupation			Number of Members of Trade Unions in Industry or Occupation			Name of Organization	Percentage Organized		
	Total	Male	Female	Total	Male	Female		Total	Male	Female
Manufacturing—(continued)										
				200	200	......	I. W. W. (Detroit).........			
				1,300	1,300	......	I. W. W. (Chicago)........			
				3,606	3,606	......	Piano Workers............			
				600	600	......	Saw Mill Workers.........			
				300	300	......	Saw Smiths...............			
				1,800	1,800	......	Timber Workers...........			
				1,170	1,170	......	Wood Carvers.............			
				3,200	3,200	......	Wood Workers............			
				2,800	2,800	......	Upholsterers.............			
Metal Industries (except Iron and Steel)...............	392,152	347,985	44,167	25,513	25,513	......		6.5	7.3	....
				10,500	10,500	......	Electrical Workers.........			
				310	310	......	Diamond Workers.........			
				2,500	2,500	......	Iron, Steel and Tin Workers			
				400	400	......	Jewelry Workers...........			
				5,435	5,435	......	Metal Polishers...........			
				612	612	......	Molders..................			
				800	800	......	Tin Plate Workers.........			
				200	200	......	Watch Case Engravers.....			
				4,636	4,636	......	West. Fed. of Miners.......			
				120	120	......	A. F. of L., local unions....			
Paper and Pulp Industries......	101,797	68,677	33,120	2,683	2,412	271		2.6	3.5	0.8
				500	500	......	Machine Printers..........			
				700	450	250	Paper Mill Workers........			
				1,400	1,379	21	Paper Makers.............			

				83	83	......	A. F. of L., local unions....			
Printing and Publishing........	249,456	200,584	48,872	85,479	79,790	5,689		34.3	39.8	11.6
				6,956	3,305	3,651	Bookbinders..............			
				1,780	1,780	......	Lithographers.............			
				900	900	......	Litho. Press Feeders.......			
				350	350	......	Lithographic Workers......			
				3,446	3,443	3	Photo Engravers...........			
				340	340	......	Poster Artists.............			
				400	400	......	Print Cutters..............			
				20,620	19,177	1,443	Printing Pressmen.........			
				45,462	44,870	592	Typographical Union.......			
				1,262	1,262	......	Steel Plate Printers........			
				100	100	......	Steel Plate Transferers.....			
				3,863	3,863	......	Stereotypers..............			
Textile Industries.............	800,251	404,368	395,883	29,862	19,377	10,485		3.7	4.8	2.6
				35	35	......	Brussels' Workers, Auburn, Mass..................			
				350	350	......	Carpet Weavers, Worcester, Mass..................			
				5,000	2,500	2,500	Cloth Weavers............			
				4,300	2,180	2,120	I. W. W. (Chicago)........			
				300	300	......	I. W. W. (Detroit).........			
				800	800	......	Lace Operatives...........			
				940	940	......	Loom Fixers..............			
				374	374	......	Machine Textile Printers...			
				127	127	......	Sailmakers' Soc. of N. Y....			
				2,746	2,746	......	Spinners.................			
				13,033	7,168	5,865	Textile Workers...........			
				134	134	......	Warpers, Philadelphia......			
				1,600	1,600	......	Woolsorters..............			
				123	123	......	A. F. of L., local unions....			

TABLE VII. — EXTENT OF ORGANIZATION AMONG PERSONS TEN YEARS OF AGE AND OVER, 1910 — *Continued*

Name of Industry or Occupation	Number of Wage Earners in Industry or Occupation			Number of Members of Trade Unions in Industry or Occupation			Name of Organization	Percentage Organized		
	Total	Male	Female	Total	Male	Female		Total	Male	Female
Manufacturing (continued)										
Miscellaneous Industries										
Broom and brush factories....	12,922	10,563	2,359	897	897	......		6.9	8.5	....
				600	600	......	Broom Makers............			
				200	200	......	Brush Makers.............			
				97	97	......	Brush Makers of N. Y......			
Button factories.............	12,879	7,748	5,131	32	32	......	A. F. of L., local unions....	0.2	0.4	....
Cigar and tobacco factories...	170,904	93,702	77,202	45,892	39,730	6,162		26.9	42.4	8.0
				41,652	37,854	3,798	Cigarmakers..............			
				3,940	1,576	2,364	Tobacco Workers..........			
				100	100	......	I. W. W. (Chicago)........			
				200	200	......	I. W. W. (Detroit).........			
Gas Works..................	22,783	22,723	60	605	605	......	A. F. of L., local unions....	2.7	2.7	....
Rubber factories............	45,864	34,059	11,805	50	50	......	A. F. of L., local unions....	0.1	0.1	....
Straw factories..............	6,458	2,377	4,081	684	684	......		10.6	28.8	....
				284	284	......	Cap Makers...............			
				400	400	......	Straw Hatters.............			
Other miscellaneous and not specified industries.........	323,534	239,128	84,406							
Transportation..................	2,890,610	2,784,581	106,029	494,662	493,702	960		17.1	17.7	0.9
Water transportation........	204,680	203,826	854	59,098	59,098	......		28.9	29.0	....
				3,108	3,108	......	Engineers.................			
				19,600	19,600	......	Longshoremen.............			
				6,000	6,000	......	Masters, Mates and Pilots..			
				9,900	9,900	......	Marine Engineers..........			
				13,800	13,800	......	Seamen...................			

				6,660	6,660	......	Steam Engineers			
				30	30	......	A. F. of L., local unions			
Construction and maintenance of streets, roads, sewers and bridges	195,793	195,443	350	4,612	4,612	......		2.4	2.4	....
				1,500	1,500	......	Pavers			
				3,070	3,070	......	Paving Cutters			
				42	42	......	A. F. of L., local unions			
Electric and street railways	154,684	154,426	258	33,773	33,773	......	Street Railway Employees	21.8	21.9	....
Teamsters and chauffeurs	748,550	748,265	285	52,128	52,128	......		7.0	7.0	....
				420	420	......	Bakery Workers			
				41,648	41,648	......	Teamsters			
				10,000	10,000	......	Teamsters, Chicago			
				60	60	......	A. F. of L., local unions			
Steam railroads	1,266,574	1,260,523	6,051	297,926	297,926	......		23.5	23.6	....
				1,000	1,000	......	I. W. W. (Chicago)			
				56,781	56,781	......	Locomotive Engineers			
				64,155	64,155	......	Locomotive Firemen			
				8,700	8,700	......	Maint. of Way Employees			
				240	240	......	Railroad Building Mechanics			
				1,100	1,100	......	Railroad Signalmen			
				600	600	......	Railroad Station Agents			
				2,180	2,180	......	Railroad Sta. Employees			
				106,343	106,343	......	Railroad Trainmen			
				3,950	3,950	......	Railroad Freight Hands			
				43,856	43,856	......	Railway Conductors			
				7,400	7,400	......	Switchmen			
				1,300	1,300	......	Tunnel Constructors			
				321	321	......	A. F. of L., local unions			
Express Companies	27,738	27,689	49							
Post	82,455	81,276	1,179	26,034	26,034	......	Letter Carriers	31.6	32.0	....

TABLE VII. — EXTENT OF ORGANIZATION AMONG PERSONS TEN YEARS OF AGE AND OVER, 1910 — *Continued*

Occupation	Number of Wage Earners in Industry or Occupation			Number of Members of Trade Unions in Industry or Occupation			Name of Organization	Percentage Organized		
	Total	Male	Female	Total	Male	Female		Total	Male	Female
Transportation (continued)										
Telegraph and telephone.......	206,561	109,562	96,999	21,091	20,131	960		10.2	18.4	1.0
				1,000	1,000	......	Commercial Telegraphers...			
				20,000	19,040	960	Railroad Telegraphers......			
				91	91	......	A. F. of L., local unions....			
Other not specified transportation......................	3,575	3,571	4							
Building Trades.................	2,480,395	2,461,652	18,743	407,174	407,174	......		16.4	16.5	....
				500	500	......	Asbestos Workers..........			
				65,311	65,311	......	Bricklayers...............			
				9,998	9,998	......	Bridge Workers............			
				6,444	6,444	......	Building Laborers..........			
				4,950	4,950	......	Carpenters, Amal..........			
				156,541	156,541	......	Carpenters, United.........			
				8,975	8,975	......	Cement Workers...........			
				600	600	......	Compressed Air Workers...			
				10,500	10,500	......	Electrical Workers.........			
				2,067	2,067	......	Elevator Constructors......			
				10,848	10,848	......	Hod Carriers..............			
				150	150	......	I. W. W. (Chicago)........			
				400	400	......	I. W. W. (Detroit).........			
				5,391	5,391	......	Lathers, Wood, Wire.......			
				105	105	......	Mosaic and Terrazzo Workers, N. Y..........			
				61,618	61,618	......	Painters..................			
				13,629	13,629	......	Plasterers................			
				24,015	24,015	......	Plumbers.................			

				1,190	1,190	......	Roofers, Composition......			
				500	500	......	Roofers, Slate and Tile.....			
				15,068	15,068	......	Sheet Metal Workers.......			
				5,600	5,600	......	Steam Fitters............			
				567	567	......	Stone Cutters............			
				1,702	1,702	......	Tile Layers..............			
				505	505	......	A. F. of L., local unions....			
Stationary Engineers............	215,053	215,043	10	9,900	9,900	......	Steam Engineers...........	4.6	4.6	....
Stationary Firemen..............	84,685	84,685	....	8,100	8,100	......	Stationary Firemen........	9.6	9.6	....
Trade..........................	1,563,117	1,181,121	381,996	15,000	12,900	2,100		1.0	1.1	0.5
Clerks and salespeople in stores.	1,308,313	938,999	369,314	15,000	12,900	2,100		1.1	1.4	0.5
Laborers.....................	254,804	242,122	12,682							
Professional Service.............	1,693,361	959,470	733,891	77,976	71,976	6,000		4.6	7.5	0.
Professional...................	1,611,695	904,422	707,273	68,760	62,760	6,000		4.3	6.9	0.8
Semi-professional..............	64,926	44,532	20,394							
Attendants and helpers.........	16,740	10,516	6,224	9,216	9,216	......		55.1	87.6	....
Domestic and Personal Service Wage Earners.................	3,185,907	960,984	2,224,923	62,719	60,747	1,972		2.0	6.3	0.1
Clerical........................	1,647,166	1,062,744	584,422	28,853	28,221	632		1.8	2.7	0,1
Bookkeepers, cashiers and accountants.................	486,700	299,545	187,155							
Clerks (except in stores)........	735,738	613,073	122,665	28,853	28,221	632		3.9	4.6	0.5
Messenger boys, etc............	108,035	96,748	11,287							
Stenographers and typists......	316,693	53,378	263,315							
Public Service..................	476,347	462,448	13,899	11,843	11,843	......		2.5	2.6	....
Agriculture Wage Earners.................	3,143,773	2,793,832	349,941							

FOOTNOTE TO TABLE VII

The figures in this table are taken from the table published in "The Extent of Labor Organization in the United States in 1910," *Quarterly Journal of Economics*, May, 1916, p. 606 and they are explained in that article. The statistics for "trade," "professional service," "domestic and personal service," "clerical workers," "public service" and "agriculture" are taken from table IV.

TABLE VIII. — EXTENT OF ORGANIZATION AMONG PERSONS TEN YEARS OF AGE AND OVER ENGAGED IN CERTAIN SELECTED OCCUPATIONS: 1920

Occupation	Number of Persons in Occupation[a]			Number of Members of Trade Unions in Occupation			Name of Organization	Percentage Organized		
	Total	Male	Female	Total	Male	Female		Total	Male	Female
Actors and showmen	48,172	33,818	14,354	19,000	11,600	7,400		39.4	34.3	51.6
				9,000	5,100	3,900	Actors and Artists			
				10,000	6,500	3,500	Vaudeville Artists			
Bakers	126,696	109,074	17,622	26,900	26,900	......	Bakery Workers	21.2	24.7	....
Barbers	182,965	182,965	....	42,700	42,700	......	Barbers	23.3	23.3	....
Blacksmiths, forgemen, and hammermen	295,313	295,313	....	51,900	51,900	......		17.6	17.6	....
				46,500	46,500	......	Blacksmiths			
				5,400	5,400	......	Horse Shoers			
Brick and stone masons	138,878	138,878	....	69,500	69,500	......	Bricklayers	50.0	50.0	....
Carpenters and joiners	892,005	892,005	....	360,900	360,900	......		40.5	40.5	....
				355,200	355,200	......	Carpenters			
				5,700	5,700	......	Lathers			
Compositors, linotypers, and typesetters	140,165	128,859	11,306	65,100	63,100	2,000	Typographical Union	46.4	49.0	17.7
Electrotypers and stereotypers	5,484	5,484	....	5,700	5,700	......	Stereotypers			
Locomotive engineers	109,899	109,899	....	80,400	80,400	......	Locomotive Engineers	73.2	73.2	....
Locomotive firemen	91,345	91,345	....	117,100	117,100	......	Locomotive Firemen			

Machinists and millwrights.......	934,102	934,102	....	316,700	316,200	500	Machinists................	33.9	33.9	....
Mail carriers....................	91,451	90,131	1,320	22,700	22,700	......		24.8	25.2	....
				22,400	22,400	......	Letter Carriers............			
				300	300	......	Letter Carriers, Rural......			
Molders, founders, casters (metal) and coremakers.............	123,668	123,668	....	53,700	53,700	......	Molders..................	43.4	43.4	....
Musicians and teachers of music...	130,265	57,587	72,678	65,000	62,400	2,600	Musicians.................			
Painters, glaziers, varnishers, enamelers and paperhangers.......	343,541	339,798	3,743	100,000	100,000	......	Painters..................	29.1	29.4	....
Pattern makers.................	27,663	27,663	......	8,400	8,400	......	Pattern Makers...........	30.3	30.3	....
Plasterers.....................	38,647	38,647	....	18,000	18,000	......	Plasterers................	46.6	46.6	....
Plumbers and gas and steam fitters.	214,101	214,101	....	71,700	71,700	......	Plumbers.................	33.5	33.5	....
Railway conductors..............	74,539	74,539	....	53,700	53,700	......		72.0	72.0	....
				52,500	52,500	......	Railway Conductors.......			
				1,200	1,200	......	Sleeping Car Conductors....			
Stationary engineers.............	242,064	242,064	....	30,000	30,000	......	Steam Engineers..........	12.4	12.4	....
Stationary firemen...............	143,862	143,862	....	28,600	28,600	......	Stationary Firemen........	19.9	19.9	....
Teachers (school)................	752,055	116,848	635,207	8,600	3,400	5,200	Amer. Fed. of Teachers.....	1.1	2.9	0.8
Teamsters......................	925,895	923,897	1,998	110,100	110,100	......	Teamsters................	11.9	11.9	....
Telephone operators..............	190,160	11,781	178,379	11,600	....	11,600	Electrical Workers.........	6.1	...	6.5

[a] Figures in these columns are taken from U. S. Census of Occupations, 1920.

TABLE IX. — EXTENT OF ORGANIZATION AMONG PERSONS TEN YEARS OF AGE AND OVER ENGAGED IN CERTAIN SELECTED OCCUPATIONS: 1910[a]

Occupation	Number of Persons in Occupation			Number of Members of Trade Unions in Occupation			Name of Organization	Percentage Organized		
	Total	Male	Female	Total	Male	Female		Total	Male	Female
Actors and showmen	48,393	35,293	13,100	9,100	7,100	2,000		18.8	20.1	15.3
				1,100	1,100	......	Actors			
				8,000	6,000	2,000	White Rats			
Bakers	117,141	105,898	11,243	18,830	18,830	......	Bakery Workers	16.1	17.8	....
Barbers	172,946	172,946	....	26,310	26,310	......	Barbers	15.2	15.2	....
Bartenders	101,234	100,984	250	25,601	25,601	......	Hotel Employees	25.3	25.4	....
Blacksmiths, forgemen, and hammermen	240,519	240,488	31	16,150	16,150	......		6.7	6.7	....
				9,000	9,000	......	Blacksmiths			
				7,150	7,150	......	Horse Shoers			
Bookbinders	39,270	18,179	21,091	6,956	3,305	3,651	Bookbinders	17.7	18.2	17.3
Brakemen	92,111	92,111	....	50,350	50,350	......		54.7	54.7	....
				900	900	......	Locomotive Firemen			
				49,450	49,450	......	Railroad Trainmen			
Brick and stone masons	169,402	169,387	15	66,179	66,179	......		39.1	39.1	....
				63,678	63,678	......	Bricklayers			
				105	105	......	Mosaic and Terrazzo Workers, N. Y.			
				567	567	......	Stonecutters			
				1,702	1,702	......	Tile Layers			
				127	127	......	A. F. of L., local unions			
Brick, tile and terra cotta workers	98,547	97,164	1,383	3,800	3,800	......	Brick Workers	3.9	3.9	....
Carders, combers and lappers	23,956	18,050	5,906	1,350	909	441	Carders, etc.	5.6	5.0	7.5

Carpenters and joiners	817,120	817,082	38	169,820	169,820	......		20.8	20.8	....
				4,950	4,950	......	Carpenters, Am. Soc. of			
				156,541	156,541	......	Carpenters, United			
				2,052	2,052	......	Railway Carmen			
				886	886	......	Shipwrights			
				5,391	5,391	......	Wood, Wire Lathers			
Compositors, linotypers, and typesetters	127,589	113,538	14,051	44,522	43,956	566	Typographical Union	34.9	38.7	4.0
Cooks	450,440	117,004	333,436	1,939	1,939	......	Hotel Employees	0.4	1.6	....
Coopers	25,299	25,292	7	4,346	4,346	......	Coopers	17.2	17.2	....
Electrotypers and stereotypers	4,368	4,268	100	3,863	3,863	......	Stereotypers	88.4	90.5	....
Glove workers	12,343	4,266	8,077	800	435	365	Glove Workers	6.5	10.2	4.5
Locomotive engineers	96,229	96,229	....	71,401	71,401	......		74.2	74.2	....
				56,781	56,781	......	Locomotive Engineers			
				14,520	14,520	......	Locomotive Firemen			
				100	100	......	Railroad Trainmen			
Locomotive firemen	76,381	76,381	....	27,938	27,938	......		36.6	36.6	....
				27,763	27,763	......	Locomotive Firemen			
				175	175	......	Railroad Trainmen			
Loomfixers	13,254	13,254	....	3,020	3,020	......		22.8	22.8	....
				940	940	......	Loomfixers			
				2,080	2,080	......	Textile Workers			
Machinists and millwrights	478,786	478,713	73	53,160	53,160	......		11.1	11.1	....
				51,900	51,900	......	Machinists			
				1,260	1,260	......	Metal Workers			
Mail carriers	80,678	79,667	1,011	26,034	26,034	......	Letter Carriers	32.3	32.7	....
Metal polishers	55,983	52,910	3,073	8,895	8,895	......	Metal Polishers	15.9	16.8	....
Molders, founders, casters (metal) and coremakers	139,215	137,262	1,953	47,050	47,050	......	Molders	33.8	34.3	....
Musicians and teachers of music	139,310	54,832	84,478	59,640	55,640	4,000				
				57,740	53,890	3,850	Musicians			
				1,900	1,750	150	Musical and Theatrical Union			

TABLE IX. — EXTENT OF ORGANIZATION AMONG PERSONS TEN YEARS OF AGE AND OVER, 1910 — *Continued*

Occupation	Number of Persons in Occupation			Number of Members of Trade Unions in Occupation			Name of Organization	Percentage Organized		
	Total	Male	Female	Total	Male	Female		Total	Male	Female
Painters, glaziers, varnishers, enamelers and paperhangers.......	362,932	359,594	3,338	63,800	63,800	......		17.6	17.7	....
				61,618	61,618	......	Painters..................			
				2,052	2,052	......	Railway Carmen...........			
				130	130	......	A. F. of L., local unions.....			
Pattern makers.................	14,869	14,775	94	5,655	5,655	......		38.0	38.3	....
				5,450	5,450	......	Pattern Makers...........			
				205	205	......	Railway Carmen...........			
Plasterers......................	47,682	47,676	6	15,262	15,262	......		32.0	32.0	....
				1,633	1,633	......	Bricklayers..............			
				13,629	13,629	......	Plasterers................			
Plumbers and gas and steam fitters	148,304	148,304	....	30,641	30,641	......		20.7	20.7	....
				24,015	24,015	......	Plumbers.................			
				1,026	1,026	......	Railway Carmen...........			
				5,600	5,600	......	Steam Fitters.............			
Potters.........................	15,591	13,536	2,055	5,680	5,582	98	Potters..................	36.4	41.2	4.8
Printers (textile)................	2,250	2,057	193	374	374	......	Machine Textile Printers...	16.6	18.2	....
Railway conductors..............	65,604	65,604	....	57,056	57,056	......		87.0	87.0	....
				200	200	......	Locomotive Firemen.......			
				43,856	43,856	......	Railway Conductors........			
				13,000	13,000	......	Railroad Trainmen.........			
Retail clerks....................	1,264,421	902,340	362,081	15,000	12,900	2,100	Retail Clerks.............	1.2	1.4	0.6
Spinners........................	74,059	27,785	46,274	5,126	5,126	......		6.9	18.4	....
				2,746	2,746	......	Spinners.................			
				2,380	2,380	......	Textile Workers, Utd.......			

Stonecutters....................	35,731	35,726	5	24,694	24,694	......		69.1	69.1	....
				13,235	13,235	......	Granite Cutters...........			
				2,458	2,458	......	Marble Workers...........			
				800	800	......	**Nat. Assn.** Stonecutters.....			
				171	171	......	**Sculptors and Carvers,** N.Y.			
				7,830	7,830	......	**Stonecutters**..............			
				200	200	......	**Stonecutters'** Soc. of N. Y..			
Switchmen, flagmen and gatemen..	73,419	73,367	52	14,275	14,275	......		19.4	19.5	....
				375	375	......	Locomotive Firemen.......			
				1,100	1,100	......	Railroad Signalmen........			
				5,400	5,400	......	Railroad Trainmen.........			
				7,400	7,400	......	Switchmen................			
Teamsters.....................	782,637	782,338	299	68,726	68,726	......		8.8	8.8	....
				420	420	......	Bakery Workers...........			
				16,448	16,448	......	Brewery Workers..........			
				150	150	......	Laundry Workers..........			
				41,648	41,648	......	Teamsters................			
				10,000	10,000	......	Teamsters of Chicago.......			
				60	60	......	A. F. of L., local unions....			
Tinsmiths, coppersmiths and solderers..................	62,621	61,774	847	16,530	16,530	......	**Sheet Metal Workers**.......	26.4	26.8	....
Upholsterers and mattress makers.	24,347	22,130	2,217	3,005	3,005	......		12.3	13.6	....
				205	205	......	Railway Carmen...........			
				2,800	2,800	......	Upholsterers..............			
Waiters........................	188,293	102,495	85,798	7,592	5,640	1,952	Hotel Employees..........	4.0	5.5	2.3
Wood carvers..................	5,315	5,257	58	1,170	1,170	......	Wood Carvers.............	22.0	22.3	....
Woolsorters and graders.........	3,576	3,102	474	1,600	1,600	......	Woolsorters...............	44.7	51.6	....

[a] The figures in this table are taken from article already cited (*Quarterly Journal of Economics*, p. 618).

INDEX

ALL reports of the National Bureau of Economic Research are critically examined in manuscript both by its scientific staff and by its Board of Directors. No report is published that has not been approved by a majority of the Board. A Director who dissents from any statement in a report approved by the majority may have his critical comments published in the report.

The present report has been reviewed in this manner and approved for publication.

The members of the Board of Directors are as follows:

NATIONAL BUREAU OF ECONOMIC RESEARCH PUBLICATIONS IN REPRINT

An Arno Press Series

Barger, Harold. **The Transportation Industries, 1889-1946:** A Study of Output, Employment, and Productivity. 1951

Barger, Harold and Hans H. Landsberg. **American Agriculture, 1899-1939:** A Study of Output, Employment, and Productivity. 1942

Barger, Harold and Sam H. Schurr. **The Mining Industries, 1899-1939:** A Study of Output, Employment, and Productivity. 1944

Burns, Arthur F. **The Frontiers of Economic Knowledge.** 1954

Committee of the President's Conference on Unemployment. **Business Cycles and Unemployment.** 1923

Conference of the Universities-National Bureau Committee for Economic Research. **Aspects of Labor Economics.** 1962

Conference of the Universities-National Bureau Committee for Economic Research. **Business Concentration and Price Policy.** 1955

Conference of the Universities-National Bureau Committee for Economic Research. **Capital Formation and Economic Growth.** 1955

Conference of the Universities-National Bureau Committee for Economic Research. **Policies to Combat Depression.** 1956

Conference of the Universities-National Bureau Committee for Economic Research. **The State of Monetary Economics.** [1963]

Conference of the Universities-National Bureau Committee for Economic Research and the Committee on Economic Growth of the Social Science Research Council. **The Rate and Direction of Inventive Activity:** Economic and Social Factors. 1962

Conference on Research in Income and Wealth. **Input-Output Analysis:** An Appraisal. 1955

Conference on Research in Income and Wealth. **Problems of Capital Formation:** Concepts, Measurement, and Controlling Factors. 1957

Conference on Research in Income and Wealth. **Trends in the American Economy in the Nineteenth Century.** 1960

Conference on Research in National Income and Wealth. **Studies in Income and Wealth.** 1937

Copeland, Morris A. **Trends in Government Financing.** 1961

Fabricant, Solomon. **Employment in Manufacturing, 1899-1939:** An Analysis of Its Relation to the Volume of Production. 1942

Fabricant, Solomon. **The Output of Manufacturing Industries, 1899-1937.** 1940

Goldsmith, Raymond W. **Financial Intermediaries in the American Economy Since 1900.** 1958

Goldsmith, Raymond W. **The National Wealth of the United States in the Postwar Period.** 1962

Kendrick, John W. **Productivity Trends in the United States.** 1961

Kuznets, Simon. **Capital in the American Economy:** Its Formation and Financing. 1961

Kuznets, Simon. **Commodity Flow and Capital Formation.** Vol. One. 1938

Kuznets, Simon. **National Income:** A Summary of Findings. 1946

Kuznets, Simon. **National Income and Capital Formation, 1919-1935:** A Preliminary Report. 1937

Kuznets, Simon. **National Product in Wartime.** 1945

Kuznets, Simon. **National Product Since 1869.** 1946

Kuznets, Simon. **Seasonal Variations in Industry and Trade.** 1933

Long, Clarence D. **Wages and Earnings in the United States, 1860-1890.** 1960

Mendershausen, Horst. **Changes in Income Distribution During the Great Depression.** 1946

Mills, Frederick C. **Economic Tendencies in the United States:** Aspects of Pre-War and Post-War Changes. 1932

Mills, Frederick C. **Price-Quantity Interactions in Business Cycles.** 1946

Mills, Frederick C. **The Behavior of Prices.** 1927

Mitchell, Wesley C. **Business Cycles:** The Problem and Its Setting. [1927]

Mitchell, Wesley C., et al. **Income in the United States:** Its Amount and Distribution 1909-1919. Volume One, Summary. [1921]

Mitchell, Wesley C., editor. **Income in the United States:** Its Amount and Distribution 1909-1919. Volume Two, Detailed Report. 1922

National Accounts Review Committee of the National Bureau of Economic Research. **The National Economic Accounts of the United States.** 1958

Rees, Albert. **Real Wages in Manufacturing, 1890-1914.** 1961

Stigler, George J. **Capital and Rates of Return in Manufacturing Industries.** 1963

Wealth Inventory Planning Study, The George Washington University. **Measuring the Nation's Wealth.** 1964

Williams, Pierce. **The Purchase of Medical Care Through Fixed Periodic Payment.** 1932

Wolman, Leo. **The Growth of American Trade Unions, 1880-1923.** 1924

Woolley, Herbert B. **Measuring Transactions Between World Areas.** 1966